SUCCESSFUL TEACHING

Tips on Psycho-teach-logy

Library of Congress Control Number: 2010906869

Published by CreateSpace
100 Enterprise Way, Suite A200
Scotts Valley, CA 95066

ISBN 1451540795 • EAN-13 9781451540796

Cover Design: *Rhenee Sarmiento and Chris Tandoc*
Editor: *Maria Esperanza Tandoc - Robles*
Assistant Editor: *Rhenee Sarmiento*

www.EdgarCiriloTandoc.com

Printed in the USA • Charleston, SC

SUCCESSFUL TEACHING

Tips on Psycho-teach-logy

Edgar Cirilo Tandoc
Author • Publisher • Philantropist

Other book by Edgar Cirilo Tandoc

"America The Beautiful"
"Our rights, responsibilities, and reflections to our free society."
ISBN 1451588143 • EAN-13 9781451588149
Available from your local bookstore
or direct from the publisher or from the author.

Or visit **www.EdgarCiriloTandoc.com**

    "**SUCCESSFUL TEACHING**" is for everyone, young or adult from all walks of life. It was written in a very simple presentation and understanding with relative ease. An inspiring piece of work that can give you the desire to read. It is a kind of material that brings about effective learning and teaching, whether you are at home, in school, in a work place, or in an outdoor park sharing good values. This book covers a wide variety of tips from complex to qualities, limitations to integrity, temperance to judgment, faith to personality, professionalism to experience, roles, legal and social status, to mention a few.

    To the non-teachers, this is also an excellent reference material where everyone can learn and understand how to nurture the love of good teaching, not just to the young ones' - but also to ourselves. The decisive question is not what methods or procedures are employed, and whether they are old-fashioned or modern, time-tested or experimental, conventional or progressive. All such considerations may be important, but none of them are ultimate, for they have something to do with the means, not the ends. And the ultimate criterion is ... result, "**A POSITIVE RESULT**."

In loving memory of my late parents

Cirilo F. Tandoc and Teresa E. Tandoc

Retired Public School Teachers

DEDICATION

This book is lovingly dedicated to my very loving, understanding, and supportive family, my children, late parents, grandparents, relatives and friends.

To my son *"Chris,"* who proudly and valiantly served in two fronts, the Operation Enduring Freedom in Iraq in 2006, and in Afghanistan in 2009 to 2010 with the elite force of the United States Marine Corps, the *Semper Fidelis.* And to those who bravely served in uniform, our heartfelt thanks.

To my first daughter *"Cathy,"* who gave me the joy of becoming a grandpa. To my gifted Aimee and Aleena, who already learned complex Math and Algebra at age eight. To my cheerers, Marc Mallbert and Ann Jollyn Sarmiento, who are both honor students.

And to all parents and grandparents, students, teachers and retirees, and aspiring teachers in both public and private school systems.

ACKNOWLEDGMENTS

There are so much to be thankful for. First and foremost, to our Almighty Creator for giving us the life and wisdom. I want to thank all those people who helped me.

I wish to give my special thanks to Rhenee Sarmiento, RN, BSN, a Masteral and Doctoral candidate, and to my son *"Chris"* of the United States Marine Corps, for their invaluable assistance in the preparation and proofreading of this book.

My *brother* Dr. Manuel Tandoc, Ph.D., a writer, lecturer, author, a retired General, and a Professor, and to my *niece* Dr. Maria Esperanza Tandoc - Robles, M.D. (OBGYN), for their profound knowledge and assistance of the relevant and valuable references.

Also, to my *brother* Dr. Erdulfo Tandoc, M.D., my *late parents,* and retired General and Dr. Jose Dalumpines, Ph.D., a *relative,* for their continued encouragements and moral support for my humble work, whose inspiring words and advices helped me become what I am now.

And to Honorable Steve Stockman, a former U.S. Congressman, U.S. House of Representatives, Washington, DC., my profound appreciation who gave me *constant* encouragement throughout this endeavor and to my *future* books.

A Very Special Thanks

A very special thanks to our world's renowned celebrity "**Jennifer Lopez**" for the fulfillment of an autographed photo, courtesy by Sony & BMG Music Entertainment sent directly to the author.

Jennifer Lynn Lopez or also known as "**J.Lo**" was born in the South Bronx, NY on July 24, 1970 to Guadalupe Rodriguez and David Lopez, both from Ponce, Puerto Rico. Jennifer's hometown was listed as Miami, Florida.

J.Lo knew from a young age that she would be a superstar one day. She has always had a love for music but was also intrigued by the film industry. Her big break in the movie was "Selena."

Jennifer married Marc Anthony on June 5, 2004, a week when Marc Anthony got divorced from Dayanara Torres, also a renowned celebrity who represented Puerto Rico in the 1993 Miss Universe and starred in thirteen movies in the Philipines and Puerto Rico.

Truly an honor, with my deepest gratitude, I shall treasure the "authographed photo" as my added collection to my library.

Psycho - teach - logy • **"Psycho"** - meaning mind or mental. **"Teach"** is how to teach the tools of the trade to new teaching and learning, or the academic skills and concepts, the quality of research. **"Logy"** - literally means science of the mind. **"Psycho-logy"** - a purely mental science. **"Psycho-teach-logy"** is a teaching and learning of the science of the mind. Inside, are the abundance of **tips**. That's how this book was born to become **"Successful Teaching"** - **"Tips on Psycho-teach-logy."**

In human relations, do not be a fault-finder,

"be a discoverer of good."

"Books are legacies that genius leaves for mankind to be learned from generation to generation, as presents to those that are yet unborn."

TABLE OF CONTENTS

PART 1
"SUCCESSFUL TEACHING"

PART 2

"THE CHILD AND HIS CURRICULUM"

Take time to read ...

it is the foundation of wisdom.

PREFACE

The birth of "**Successful Teaching**" for new teachers. Formulated by the author after careful and extensive research, this work however, is by no means complete. It is only the beginning of a book the author intends to publish. To better serve the purpose, this work is divided in two parts.

Part 1 "Successful Teaching"

Part 2 "The Child and His Curriculum"

The author cannot too warmly express his special gratitude to the most beloved, understanding, and special friend Rhenee Sarmiento, a Registered Nurse (RN) with a Bachelor of Science in Nursing (BSN), and Dr. Maria Esperanza Tandoc - Robles, MD, for their varied and progressive contribution to Education and for their continued moral support and encouragement; *to my late parents,* for providing the materials on the Child and His Curriculum which they compiled during a lifetime of teaching in the Bureau of Public Schools. It is the author's earnest desire that this book may *contribute* in one way or the other to the development of better teachers on whose shoulders will lay the grave responsibility of educating our people for better citizenry.

"Part 1"

"Successful Teaching"

THE TEACHER

As a teacher, one should be the master of the situation, not easily annoyed or angered. Because teaching demands consecrated lives and the time and energies of the most gifted, a teacher must be devoted, prompt, courteous and dignified, firm, natural, prepared, just, active, tactful, progressive and up-to-date.

Teachers who find much trouble with the discipline of unpleasing and forceful personality should look out for a remedy or quit the business of teaching. Otherwise, he should be confident of himself that he can talk in low, decisive tone without threat or bluster even under the most trying circumstances.

Teaching involves teachers and parents in education. In the case of primary and secondary education, parents bring their children to school expecting the teachers to take care of them while they are at work. Most parents spend their time at work that parental involvement in the school is always a problem raised by teachers and some parents too. Teachers, on the other hand, expect parents to get involved in school activities and give their share in shaping and forming their children.

In ranking the expectations of the parents and the teachers as to their respective roles, fathers and mothers expect their teachers to:

" ... *be a good example to the children, teach the children, care and love the children.*"

While teachers on the other hand, expect parents to:

" ... *teach the children good manners and right conduct, express their care and love for the children, and teach the children to respect their teachers.*"

Both parents and teachers believed that they can mold the children effectively by:

"... *having an open line of communication, supporting each other while working as a team and providing an honest feedback regarding the children's progress.*"

Based on the findings of the study, communication ranked first. As a team, supporting each other, they can work together in teaching the children good manners and right conduct. Therefore, teaching to be effective is always accompanied with love and care.

THE CHEERFUL TEACHER

Teaching is a noble profession. A selfless teacher toiling uncompromisingly, diligently, honesty in abnegation makes ours a happy world.

At dawn break, this meek molder of man's character faces the day with renewed faith and enthusiasm in his noble mission to develop the character and enlighten the mind of the youth of the land.

At dusk, when the day's work becomes a prelude to another, a teacher smiles with pride and in solid contentment for he has unselfishly contributed his just share to the cause of public service.

In the deep silence of the night, burns his midnight candle for the next lesson plan that will forge man's primitive instincts on the anvil of learning and equal opportunity.

Within the four walls of the classroom, he radiates with wisdom, understanding and sympathy. By destiny, he is a maker of future citizens.

And like the Savior, never swayed by misgivings, *"never awed by opinion, never seduced by flattery, undismayed by disaster,"* a cheerful teacher lead a full life of love, courage, faith, and hope.

A teacher has every reason to be cheerful. He has a divine mission to accomplish. A teacher has a beautiful love. All honor him!

SHALL I BE A TEACHER?

It is well for you to pause now and take an inventory of yourself and your potentialities. Do you measure up to the task before you? Can you ever become a successful teacher?

Before you attempt to answer the above questions, special attention must be given to the problems of teachers and their handicaps in imbedding sound citizenship training and high moral and ethical principles which are contributory factors to a great movement of national unity through educational process.

Choosing teaching as a vocation is like deciding where to go on a vacation. The obvious difference, of course, is that selecting a profession is a serious matter. If one is planning on a vacation, he must first decide what kind of a vacation he wants to have.

A vacation trip involves planning. It includes breaking up the trip into sections; determining how far to go in one day; selecting in advance the spots where to stop and rest. This is also true in planning common-sense approach to the selection of a teacher's goal.

First of all, he should ask why he enrolled himself in the college of education; whether he has the necessary aptitude to work for the ends of education; whether he has the personality and qualifications required of a teacher more so to be in the society of the young.

SUCCESS IN TEACHING

Success in teaching is not given but earned, not granted but merited. So that hard work and industry and ones native talents must go together if one aims at successful teaching. A good teacher is tireless in his quest for wisdom, who stresses not so much on authority but on responsibility, not so much on power but on service.

The young teacher, therefore, endowed with the missionary zeal in educating the masses, must utilize his undaunted service to improve the cause of education in its insatiable search for truth, learning and culture.

Success in teaching is available to everyone. There is no magic formula for it. It is simply a question of making the most of what his talents and abilities can do.

COMPLEX JOB OF TEACHER

A teacher carries a tremendous responsibility and has an exceeding complicated job. For instance, he is expected to be a psychologist; he is an untiring counselor in imparting knowledge to the students of whom he is responsible, socially and morally.

As a teacher, he should be understanding and patient. A teacher should always bear in mind that education is a continuous process and as such he should see to it that the students learn according to the utmost standard expected of them; so that when they go out into the world after graduation, they are prepared and molded in such way as to be able to face the challenges in life.

"Education is defined as the full and harmonious development of all the faculties or powers of man - the physical, mental, and moral - to prepare him here and hereafter."

A teacher should be aware of the *"individual differences"* of students. That is, in order to understand them, he must know how to put himself in the place of the students. After all, he was a student himself before he became a teacher.

In most instances, students show more similarity than

dissimilarity. Within certain limits students have equal physical needs and spiritual cares. These needs should be satisfied if they are to live a well-balanced life. A teacher should think of his students as extraordinary intricate beings. So that he must employ all his knacks and tacks in dealing with them.

QUALITIES OF A GOOD TEACHER AND CLASSROOM PROBLEMS

Students behavior vary from one another and from time to time. Sometimes happy and at times sad. This is true from day to day. So, in order to understand their behavior better, the teacher should keep in mind that there is always a reason for their actions; why a student does or says something, or thinks about something. Generally, thought precedes a student's words or actions.

Science teaches us that for every stimulus there is a response. Students' thoughts and actions are difficult to understand but stimulus-response or cue action explanation can be used best to explain some of their behavior. To understand these better, a teacher should be primarily concerned with *"why"* of their behavior. If a teacher can find out the reasons for them, he can change such indifference into acceptance. In analyzing all this, a teacher may find that their indifference is caused either by an act with knowledge or by some social problems in school or at home. But understanding alone is not enough; a teacher must also endeavor to help them.

The desire to lead is an important component of the ability to deal with students. As a rule, there are two kinds of students - the most dominant and the submissive. It is imporant to note, however, that teachers need not be selected from the very dominant end of the range.

"The fundamental standard of the teacher's success is the improvement of those who come under his or her influence."

"It is generally agreed all teachers should have a broad outlook on life and a rich cultural background."

LIMITATION AND INTEGRITY

A teacher's recognition of his own fallibility is another important aspect of the ability to deal with students. The arrogant teacher who considers his students only as cogs is apt to endanger resentnent in his classroom which is not conducive to effective learning.

Integrity is a *"sine qua non"* for a teacher. The lack of integrity can never be concealed for very long. Once students lose confidence in their teacher's integrity, a good student-teacher relationship is difficult to restore. There are some unfortunate students who have deep-rooted fear. They dread to talk; they dread the possibility that others may make derogatory remarks about them. In this aspect, the teacher must endeavor to avoid or help minimize the situation because this group of students will find it hard to adjust themselves even after they finish schooling.

Sine qua non or **sine qua non** was originally a Latin legal term for *"(a condition) without which it could not be"* or *"but for ..."* or *"without which (there is) nothing."* It refers to an indispensable and essential action, condition, or ingredient.

TEMPERANCE

For establishing really effective relationship with students, a teacher must have a realistic attitude towards them. It should be borne in mind that no human being is thoroughly good; that students have their own shortcomings and weaknesses, or even teachers for that matter. A well-adjusted temperance or temperament of a teacher in the school room is an essential factor to better student-teacher relationship. An indignant teacher is apt to develop fear in the student, rather than love or affection in the latter's work. Over meekness and liberty to students will in turn spoil classroom harmony.

A teacher who insults his students for not knowing his lesson, more often than not, make the latter shrink into indifference in his pursuits, not to mention the hatred that might be implanted in his heart. It will be noteworthy to remember that students have diverse mental capacities, excluding the environmental problems of his social life, which may also be responsible for his failure to attend thoroughly to his classroom responsibilities. A teacher who finds it *"fun"* to embarrass his student may be educated but not cultured. And education without culture is a black eye to the ends of education.

"Education is growth. I may not often see your face or hear your voice, but through the intervals our thoughts entwine - and I am richer, stronger, for your love, O teacher, friend of mine."

JUDGMENT

The teacher must exercise good judgment in all facets of his job. Judgment is clearly related to intelligence, but is not identical with it. It is related to experience as well but again not perfectly. It is probable that its relation to experience stems largely from two factors. First, the more information a teacher knows about the problem, the better in his judgment. Second, experience of certain actions in a particular situation. Good judgment must go hand in hand with speed in decision-making. A good decision made too late may be worse than a poor decision made at an appropriate moment. Indecision and vacillation are crippling. The most valuable teacher is not he who never makes mistakes, but he who makes decisions with all necessary speed and whose judgment is sufficiently good that relatively few of the decisions are wrong.

Finally, a teacher must possess physical vitality. The work is so demanding and tremendous that a lethargic person simply cannot keep pace with it. He must be strong and full of vigor otherwise he becomes submissive, which is not desirable for a teaching job. He will let breaches of discipline pass and will fail to stand up for things that should be defended because he does not care to expand the effort to deal with the situation.

PUBLIC RELATIONS AND PERSONALITY DEVELOPMENT IN TEACHING

Many a teacher has confined his pedagogic preoccupation within the four walls of the classroom disregarding altogether and showing little interest if at all his association with people in the community.

Perhaps, we might say, he should not be blamed for this isolationist attitude because of the nature of his profession which demands that he, so he thinks, be that way. But then it should be remembered that a teacher's mission extends beyond the proverbial four corners of the classroom. On the contrary, it should and must be gregarious in its approach if it is to reap the most of its effectiveness. One thing, however, remains - that he should not lose his identity in the maze of personalities so that he can still cling to the foundation of dignity that strongly supports his profession.

"Education is life."

"A fundamental feature of the work of teaching is to be found in the very attitudes of the teachers themselves."

The importance of public relations as observed and practiced by teachers cannot be overemphasized and be dismissed lightly without sacrificing the ideals and tenets on which their avocation is firmly founded. For one thing it cannot be gainsaid that a teacher as such should exert some effort in having his influence felt in whatever community activity which requires school participation. Here is where his public relations are put to a test. It is on occasions like this when a teacher's ways of getting along with the people make or break his cordial relationships with this constituents in the community. It determines whether he earns or loses their high regard for him as one to look up to when they feel that his intercession is called for. In other words, a mentor is to elicit the spontaneous and unsolicited cooperation in the formidable task of rearing the students in school, he in turn is more than expected to give them a hand in their just reasonable needs as well when the opportune time comes.

Thus it is not idle to say that aloofness or indifference on the teacher's part is his own undoing as far as the success in molding the young mind and the tender in years is concerned.

A teacher is a human being. And as much he has the human instinct of being gregarious. He seeks company. In his association with people a social cohabitation exists which develops his ways, attitudes and character combined, to give birth, fertilize, mold and project his personality.

A teacher is expected to exercise due discretion in upholding his principles as a genuine mentor whenever they run contrary to that of the people. By all means he must hold on *(if we may add)* stubbornly to what he believes is right. On some occasions, however, compromise is in order for as long as it affects the common good. It is to be understood in any way not to give in to everybody's desire and pleasure. This impossibility and futility will break him apart.

To some extent a teacher is judged by the public eye by his actuations in front of them. It is believed that a healthy personality cannot be projected and transmitted by a teacher who does not have it in the first place.

"The excellent teacher maintains a friendly and helpful attitude towards all others at all times."

A TOUCHING STORY OF A TEACHER

"Good-bye Mr. Chips" one of James Hamilton's best seller gives us a touching story of a teacher who molded young lives and gave his utmost task.

On his deathbed, Mr. Chips heard a remark *"tis a pity, he never had any children."*

The old man roused himself and with his eyes glistening murmured: *"Children? Why, I have had more of them than any parent I know. Thousands of 'em"* - his voice tailed off while living memories thronged into the room. The generations he had served rose up to call him blessed. He had lived a full life, and success was on his face as he passed away.

We find a simple and wholesome message in the story, especially those of us who are teachers. We may not have natural children but only spiritual ones. At death, we too, want those spiritual children to rally around us and cheer us with the rest that carry on our mission. The teacher is likened to an apostle. So much is expected by his subjects. An apostle is one who is sent. A teacher is sent for the salvation of his students. It may not directly be missionary's task; nevertheless, it is bound to lead to the same goal.

It does not suffice that a teacher have knowledge; he ought to have virtue as well, it is not enough that he be sane - that he is mentally aware of reality, capable of seeing what is there to see; he must likewise, be saintly - namely, loyal in his concrete conduct, to that awareness of reality, consistent with what he sees.

"Learning increases in apt and vivid communication; and communication and discussion are indelible mark of civilized and humanistic society. From this wise, learning becomes fruitfully contagious."

The teacher, as an apostle must have a code and must live by it. As an *"uncanonized"* the teacher remains steadfastly loyal to the doctrine and practice of moral living. Virtue becomes a must in a teacher. The student is, by nature and inclination, a born hero-worshipper. And the teacher topples down in the estimation of his students, so also will all his educational efforts go overboard. For he will be despised; he will not be heard.

Such is the case, then, of an educator that is not virtuous. He is either shunned or despised. And in this he is a failure as an apostle, and should not be emulated in his wrong doings, because he would have brought a greater disaster to his mission, and to the souls entrusted to him.

A TEACHER'S PERSONAL QUALITIES

A teacher is both born and made. Success in teaching is the result of painstaking study and a determined effort to acquire attitudes and develop skills and other teaching competencies. Here are the following competencies of teachers:

1) He must love his profession and grow in it.

2) He must love and understand children.

3) He must love work and should be ready to do more than is ordinarily expected of him.

4) He must believe in the inherent goodness of man. He must be an optimist.

5) He must possess a personal philosophy. He must know what his mission in life is.

6) He must possess an ideal.

7) He must develop a pleasant personality, try to be attractive and be emotionally adjusted.

8) He must be physically and mentally fit.

9) He must help improve life in the community.

10) He must live a clean and moral life.

THE SPIRITUAL MAN
AND EDUCATION

In the field of scholastic philosophy in education, a teacher, in order to understand fully his students as men of physical and spiritual existence, a teacher should attempt to know all that he can learn about them.

The new-born child is the product of all that has come in the biological history of both parents. A teacher should attempt to know all about him. He grows. He acquires his first education at home. He goes to school. He becomes formally educated.

"I would rather stand alone in a conscious pride than err with millions on my side."

The home and the school are agencies responsible for the growth and development of the child. Education plays an important role in his being a rational animal, called man. Man is of physical existence. He is endowed with reasons. His physical existence is called the body; his reasons - the mental, the intellect or the thing called soul. Man is a being of two composite parts: the material object, the body, and the non-material object, the soul.

Some exponents in education explain man's ultimate aim in education *"ends up in society."* We suppose that man has spiritual property - the soul. With the physical, both must undergo the process of development. Education, therefore, is the full and harmonious development of the faculties or powers of man: the physical, mental, moral - the latter referring to both the natural and supernatural order. By faculties or powers is meant, in mental education, the intellect, the imagination, the will, and sensitive appetite. The emotion enters into education as an exercise of the will and sensitive appetite, governed by the supreme faculty, the intellect. By harmonious development, we mean a well-proportioned development, without lopsidedness or distortion. A man is not harmoniously developed for instance, if he is a perfect muscular specimen with a defective brain; or if he is a mental genius without morality in the natural or supernatural sphere.

Teachers who are not familiar with the range and depth of Scholastic Philosophy in Education will today object to the idea of faculty education. By faculty education means the speculative scientific knowledge, coupled with wisdom - as outlined in the scheme of the speculative sciences and the expression of that science and wisdom in a practical external way.

Therefore, a student must be educated both physically and spiritually. It is this training that makes him understand that he has a body which can be developed; a mind that enables him to make use of all the elements of nature to discover new things beneficial for the human race. And above all, a soul that makes him feel the call of things spiritual and prepares him to serve and love that *"Supreme Being"* and his fellowmen. This kind of education produces students with the developed body, sound mind and well-nourished soul. Sometimes we pay so much attention to the development of our body and mind neglecting our soul. If our body needs to be cleaned, washed, clothed, and be fed to live - our soul needs much more washing and must be fed not materially but spiritually.

THE CONCEPT OF EDUCATION

What is education?

Education is regarded in two *senses:* as a product and as a process; a product because it is the result of experience and a process; because it is a process, a social process through which and by which the experience of the race such as knowledge, skills, and attitudes are transmitted to the members.

"He who would accomplish things must toughen his hide to the darts of criticism, because some people laugh at us, while others doubt our ability or sincerity, we can't afford to stop trying."

PERSONALITY TRAITS

An excellent teacher not only is approachable, but improves his methods of meeting people. He has a convincing speech and pleasing address. He greets people pleasantly and makes his first impressions favorably. An excellent teacher exudes with dignity or reservation which is maintained without coldness, stiffness, or offensiveness. He carries an excellent bearing before the class, with poise and modesty. There is the reasoned and dignified quietness and confidence. He balances friendliness with dignified reserve, which he maintains regularly. He maintains enthusiasm and pep in the schoolroom.

He is painstakingly and consistently fair and impartial with the pupils in opportunity, in giving, in grading and in decisions. He upholds to the principle of fairness.

An excellent teacher is a genuine scholar and has a broad general education. His scholarship is a power in his hands in helping him prevent disorder, command confidence, secure and hold attention, inspire faithful service, and set up ideals to be attained. His scholarship is not static, but progressive.

He attempts to live the hygiene and the morality he teaches. He is not only sincere, but friendly and tactful, as well as firm and certain. He is not only sincere in attitude and purpose but practices sincerity in dealing with pupils. He is what he teaches. He is sincere in all his human relationship.

An excellent teacher has sympathy with each of his pupils. He can put himself in their places and see things from their points of view, as well as from that of society.

An excellent teacher is characterized by an unmistakable courtesy in both attitude and action. He not only teaches courtesy, but practices it as well.

An excellent teacher is generous even at fault. He is in a state of readiness to forgive. His actions are not confined more to duty, but are characterized by service over and beyond the requirements of the contract. He is generous of his service to the country.

TEACHER'S PROFESSIONAL BACKGROUND

A teacher should understand that teaching is a noble profession involving years of preparation. A profession differs from a trade and a calling in that the former takes not only years to prepare but that it also is guided by fundamental principles.

Teaching law, medicine, engineering are professions. But carpentry, auto-mechanics, locksmithing, plumbing, etc. are trades which could be acquired in a few months of time. Mere attendance in schools or colleges for education however does not assure one of success in the teaching profession. It is the kind and quality of preparation that the student did himself. It includes the facts and knowledge concerning the student, namely, the learning that he acquired, the skills and techniques he mastered, the formation of habits and attitudes, and lastly, the ideals that he gained. All these matter the most.

PRE-TEACHING EXPERIENCE

No teacher's training can be considered adequate if it does not include a carefully planned pre-teaching laboratory expe-rience in and off-campus. Teachers must not only know their principles of teaching but should be able to apply them to actual teaching-learning experience.

THE TEACHER'S ROLE
IN THE CLASSROOM

The teacher has a definite function to do not only in the classroom but also outside of it. He is a guide, a leader, and a parent to his students.

The valuable information to remember leading to the role of the teachers in the classroom are as *follows:*

1) The teacher is a director of learning rather than a listener of lesson. By this, it means that the modern classroom emphasizes cooperative group planning by both the teacher and the students. The recitation has become a free discussion of what each student feels and believes what is right and should be done. Each student contributes his share in the common enterprise. He studies books but does not *"parrot them verbatim"* to satisfy the capricious whim of the teacher. The teacher guides the learning activity but does not require students to memorize unrelated facts. Instead, he carefully draws out their ideas by a skillful manipulation of the learning situation so that the student does not mistake one thing for another.

2) A teacher should always give the student the benefit of the doubt. It is not always possible to fathom the motivation of the student. He often gets into trouble for flimsy causes. While serious disturbances should not be allowed to go on unnoticed, it would be better to give the student to a chance to do better especially when the teacher is in doubt as to the strength of his guilt. *"Nagging and scolding for poor lessons and threatening pupils with failures are not signs of excellence in teaching."*

3) Every teacher should take time to become well acquainted with a new class of students before making any major assignment. The making of assignments should never be made mechanical and routinely.

Every new assignment should be a new challenge to both the students and the teacher. And this cannot be done unless the teacher has become well acquainted first with his pupils.

4) Regardless of the length of one's experience, no teacher should enter a classroom without a lesson plan prepared for that specific class and for a specific purpose. The lesson plan is still and perhaps will always be indispensable to the teacher no matter what his training and experience is. Lesson plans need not be elaborate and detailed. Lesson plan serves as a guide in the

teaching-learning activity which no teacher can afford without.

5) Classroom procedures should not resemble a contest in which the teacher is pitted against the student. The question-and-answer technique often shows the presence of a tendency to mark the boundary between an *"all-knowing"* teacher and a *"know-nothing"* student. Tricky questions often are asked to transgress a student or to show where he falters. This is not psychological and is totally uncalled for.

6) Techniques of teaching should be the slaves of teaching rather than teachers being the slaves of techniques. Teachers should always ask themselves *"why they do this or why they do that."* In so doing they are reminded of their goals which justify the methods they use. A method is used to realize an aim. To be effective it must realize that aim.

7) Discipline is something more than good classroom order. Discipline should not be confused with order. The modern concept of discipline emphasizes self-control instead of an imposed control from without. Order connotes the presence of authority imposed from outside.

"Foresight is better than hindsight."

8.) In the classoom just as in any larger unit of democracy there can be no freedom without responsibility. A teacher in a democratic school does not award freedom to an individual student, rather he enables him to achieve freedom through proper social interaction.

"Freedom is earned in exchange of responsibility."

In school, the student is free to move about the room, going to and back as may be indicated. But in return, he assumes the responsibility of proper behavior. All students do not achieve their freedom at the same time and in the same degree although the rights to freedom are equal in the beginning.

CONCEPTS OF EDUCATION AS DEFINED BY DIFFERENT AUTHORS

a) Development of the whole man.

b) Development of moral character.

c) Development of free enlightened personality.

d) The formation of habits.

e) Preparation for complete living.

f) Many-sized interest.

g) Self-realization.

h) Preparation for ordinary duties of life.

i) Development of character.

j) Dominance of man over things.

k) Development of all the powers.

l) To dispel error and to discover truth.

m) Attainment of virtue in the individual.

n) Attainment of happiness through perfect virtue.

o) Advancement of human knowledge.

p) Attainment of sound mind in the sound body.

q) Mastery of tools indispensable to the race.

r) Understanding the world in which one lives.

"Philosophy of education is an integrated system of values that serves as a guide to one's thinking and conduct. It is a way of interpreting life."

Everything that happens today may be attributed to the kind of education that the youth of the land are subjected to. If it had brought peace and order to society, we can rightfully say that the present educational process is on the right track. But if chaos dominates social groups and crime waves are surging high, we cannot help but feel that something is wrong somewhere; and that we always look at education as the strong influence on the mind and character of the young. As such, it is at this point that we desire to concentrate our efforts in the hope that we can contribute in no small measure to the total development of a society we desire to live in.

We believe that there is a need to reorient ourselves on the strategies and processes that make up our system of education. Maybe this is a tall order but in the meantime, as a starting avenue toward some higher educational endeavors we try to retrieve from old files of educational tools, a pack of stories and legends useful in our humble desire to infuse character development among the students in this highly technological age.

TEACHER'S RELATIONS
WITH THE STUDENTS

A teacher should know not only his rights but also the rights of his students. The students' place in school is governed by certain laws and by rules and regulations based on laws.

"Education is the result of the interaction between the individual and his environment. It is a continuous process of experiencing and of revising experiences. It is change, growth, life."

The students have *"legal"* as well as *"social"* status. They are as *follows:*

LEGAL STATUS

1) Individuals are entitled to at least a free elementary education. In practice, there is free primary education in the Bureau of Public Schools. One cannot be deprived of admission to public school if he has attained seven (7) years of age. This is his legal right if there are available facilities like room, teacher,

funds, *et cetera*. This right may not apply if he has physical and mental defects that will not qualify him from doing well in school.

SOCIAL STATUS

Once enrolled, this individual assumes a social status. From it, he assumes his proper place in school as befit a member in a social group. The duty of the teacher is to see to it that all those enrolled are assured of acceptance in it. And in order to do this, it calls for true understanding of them.

2) Once enrolled, his school attendance is a combination of privilege, right and obligation. Attendance in school is a privilege. And once the proper conditions concerning age, residence and availability of space are met, it becomes a right. Once enrolled and accepted, the student is obliged to attend school regularly and to obey all school rules and regulations promulgated by its competent authorities.

3) There are two (2) kinds of absence, the *legal* and the *illegal*. An enrolled individual is legally absent if he is sick, if someone is sick in the family where his services are mostly needed, if he lacks clothing, or the weather is inclement so that his life is

in danger if he goes to school. Legal absence is excusable. Illegal absence includes truancy, willful absence without valid cause, like attending fiestas and other celebrations in other places and the like.

4) No child nor parent need pay extra payments for instruction done in school. Teachers are prohibited from accepting directly and indirectly for tutorial services other than the compensation authorized for his services as a teacher.

"Education is the ever recurring opportunity of society to correct its mistakes."

5) The child is entitled to a *just, fair,* and *impartial* treatment from his teachers. Prejudice or discrimination because of difference in the students' mental equipment, social standing, or favors granted by parents has no place in school.

6) An enrolled individual *(pupil as commonly applied)* is entitled to security, mentally or physically. Corporal punishments in any form or manner while still legally permissible to some extent *"in loco parents" (in the place of parents)* is totally prohibited by school regulations. This individual is entitled to respect of his personality and integrity. He should not be ridiculed or shamed in the class.

7) Every child is entitled to the acceptance of his social group. Belongingness or group acceptance is a necessary pre-requisite to proper emotional adjustment. The newcomer must be helped in acquiring and accepting friends.

8) The teacher's biggest challenge comes from the true recognition of the child's worth. In a true democracy, every individual is entitled to a recognition of his worth and dignity, whatever his origin, color or present status. The handicapped, the dull, the average child and the superior child, all have equal chances to make good and be consistent with their own abilities. No one needs to be disliked by the teacher because of birth, or low mental ability.

9) Faith in human nature is essential to teaching. Children should be trained to accept responsibilities for good behavior. The teacher does not need to warn his pupils that dire consequences will befall him who does wrong. Instead, he should encourage them to do right. Suspiciousness on the part of the teacher is uncalled for.

10) No two individuals *(pupils)* are alike. No two individuals react to the same situations in exactly the same way. Neither does he respond in the same manner to the situation in

two different settings. The test of the teacher is therefore to understand each of them so that the best in him is developed.

"Reflection rather than rush action is his rule."

11) Every normal child is not always himself all the time. Normal children often misbehave not because they have become bad but because in the process of learning, lapses are bound to take place.

12) Every child desires praise, acceptance, and success. School tasks must present a challenge but the child must be allowed to succeed if he were to keep his ego and therefore his self-worth and dignity.

CONCLUSION

Finally, a teacher must know what learning is. He must know how an individual learns, what makes him learn or fail to learn, and the conditions most favorable for maximum learning.

There can be no teacher without a learner, although there may be learning without a teacher. The pupil, the student, the learner, or whatever you may call them is the *"raison d'etre"* of teaching. And learning is the purpose of all teachings. Learning, being both a process and a product may be fully learned by you in the course you are now taking or have taken in the College of Education.

"Education is the attainment of social competence and optimum individual development."

❏ ❏ ❏

Raison d'être is a phrase borrowed from French meaning simply, *"reason for being"*. In English, it also comes to suggest a degree of rationality, *"The claimed reason for the existence of something or someone"*.

TEACHER'S PERSONAL EVALUATION

As an ideal teacher: Please answer Yes or No

1) Do you have the necessary intelligence to do excellent college work and profit from four / five years of teacher education?

_____

2) Does your personality make you a suitable companion for children?   _____

3) Do you find enjoyment in the society of children?   _____

Students?   _____

4) Do you have a sound body and an abundance of health and energy?   _____

5) Do you have high moral and religious ideals?   _____

6) Are you willing to prepare yourself thoroughly for teaching by acquiring the knowledge, skills, and appreciations necessary for successful teacher?   _____

7) Do you find happiness in such things as good looks, good music, and beautiful pictures?   _____

8) Do you like people and can you live in harmony with an ordinary community? _____

9) Are you interested in community activities? _____

10) Are you open-minded and tolerant with the views of others?

_____

11) Do you have enough patience to listen to the endless questions that children ask? _____

12) Do you believe that human nature is disposed towards the good? _____

13) Do you have a desire for self-improvement? _____

14) Do you have a well-balanced sense of humor? _____

15) Do you live a clean and moral life? _____

*If all your answers are favorable, then you are an ideal teacher. Carry on, be "**honest**" to yourself, and Good Luck!*

All of us, deep in our hearts, wish to speak the truth. We want to be sincere in thoughts and in deed. We want to be steadfast, contended, and sportsmanlike in all our dealings with other people.

Honesty is a good beginning for all of this. Unless we

can trust one another and accept what our friends say as true, we live in a worried state of mistrust and suspicion.

Honesty of the heart and of the mind is called *"sincerity."* True honesty is always sincere. Acting honestly, trying sincerely to do our very best, never cheating, and accepting defeat cheerfully and gallantly is *"good sportsmanship."* Looking for the honest and sincere beauty in simple homely things and finding happiness in our humble, everyday surroundings, are what lead us to one of the greatest of all human gifts, *"contentment."*

"If we encounter a man of rare intellect, we should ask him what books he has read?"

Modern concept and democratic one.

"Interest is a feeling of value."

"Education may be formal or informal."

"Reading is to the mind what exercise is to the body."

2

INTRODUCTION

If you are convinced that you possess the necessary qualifications to become a teacher, you may be interested in some of the additional information concerning teaching as a profession. *They are listed below:*

1) Knowledge about children, their individual differences in mental age, ability, interest and sex, and in comprehension and speed in learning of previous training.

2) Ability to measure the results of teaching by the use of standard tests.

3) The concept on how the minds of pupils function in learning the subject matter or acquiring the skill - the fundamental laws of learning.

4) Familiarity with the aims, functions, and purposes of education in social progress.

5) Knowledge of the historical development of the

modern schools as social institutions and its relation to other social institutions of today.

6) Knowledge of the organization of education - units of administation and methods of control.

7) Knowledge of the relation of subject - matter to the needs of the child and to the needs of society, the relation of the subject matter to the aims and functions of education.

8) Working knowledge of the various ways of presenting subject - matter, the various types of classroom procedure - inductive and deductive, objective, socialized appreciation, drill, and review.

9) Knowledge of the problem of controlling the behavior and conduct of the pupils in school - understanding of proper standards of conduct according to the age of the pupils and school conditions; understanding of rational measures of discipline that are adequate to maintain the standard set up.

10) Knowledge of physical defects prevalent among school children, and methods of preventing and detecting them.

THE CHILD AND HIS CURRICULUM

The Child

What is a child? A child is defined as a young person of either sex at any age less than maturity, but most commonly one between infancy and youth.

"Birth makes the arrival but not the true commencement of an individual. The life career of an individual begins with conception, when the genes of father and mother unite and initiate a cycle of growth. A minute globule of protoplasm becomes an embryo, the embryo becomes a fetus, the fetus an infant, the infant a child."

When these parent cells unite, much of what the individual is to be is determined. The new-born child is the product of all that has come before in the biological history of both parents. Modern education attempts to know all that it can learn about the child. It is but natural then that we should ask concerning the new-born child. What does he bring into the world with him that will be of value to know education?

Each child comes into the world with a complete nervous system and its appropriate receptors. Reflexes would not be possible without such mechanism. If something is suddenly thrust towards the eyes, they close, with no conscious thought in doing. This is reflex. The eye is the receptor. It receives the light waves that come from the moving object; the nervous system transmits the message; and the muscles of the eyelids cause them to close. For all reflexes we have this type of combination of receptor, a transmitting organ, and a reacting mechanism. The eyes, the ears and other parts of the body, that are usually called the sense organs, are all receptors.

In addition to these should be added many receptors in and under the skin, and in the organs within the body. The beginning of each reflex is in one of these receptors. A pin suddenly thrust into the body touches a pain receptor under the skin and starts the reflex that ends in a sudden movement of the body. There is much discussion among psychologists as to what extent such reflexes are inborn.

For purposes of our study in this course we need not be troubled with such question. We know that reflexes exist long before the teacher comes in contact with the child. Reflexes are of value in education. Most of them are concerned with the preservation of the body and the secretion of glands that aid in the bodily functions. Food causes the flow of saliva and onions bring tears to the eyes; both are important but not subject to education.

Instincts

Instinct is a controversial subject, because there are many differences of opinion about it. It is difficult to find two psychologists who agree as to what they are. On one extreme are those who deny the very existence of instincts. On the other extreme are those who base a whole psychological theory upon it. In books written during the last decade, many new expressions have been used by psychologists to take the place of the word instinct.

In an outline such as this, it is impossible to discuss all the schools of psychology and the attitude of each concerning instinct. If such a task were attempted it would be necessary to deal with behaviorism, Gestalt psychology, psychoanalysis, purposivism, dynamic psychology, functional psychology, and a great many others. Such a discussion is valuable but must be left to a course devoted to educational psychology.

The last section dealt with reflexes, which are simple, unlearned reactions, such as sneezing and knee jerkings. Something happens to a receptor and the results come immediately and without thought. If conditions are made more complex by introducing new factors, and if the resultant behavior is unlearned and common to the race, it can be said to be instinctive. Basically, instincts differ from reflexes only in complexity. Some psychologists say there is no such thing as *"unlearned"* and that all activities are due to learning. Such psychologists prefer to use the term *"prepotent"* reflexes. Some call them universal habits. Other psychologists prefer to think of a drive which leads to action that is inborn. It is unwise for us to attempt to enter upon a discussion of this point. Whether these activities are learned or unlearned every possible use should be made of them in education.

Classifications of Instincts

Since many psychologists deny the existence of instincts, our classification should begin by the recognition of this fact. Those who do recognize instincts classify them in many ways.

First Classification

Threefold Classification of Instincts

1) Responses to organic needs - *examples:*

a) thirst

b) hunger

c) breathing

d) heat and cold

e) shrinking from injury

f) crying

g) fatigue

h) rest and

i) sleep

2) Responses to other persons - *examples:*

a) herd or gregariousness instinct

b) mating

c) parental or mothering instinct

3) Responses to play - *example:*

a) locomotion

b) vocalization

c) manipulation

d) submission

e) docility

"Instincts are native or unborn reaction tendencies."

Professor William McDougall of Duke University gives the following lists of *instincts:*

1) The instinct to escape from danger, with the accompanying emotion of fear.

2) The instinct of combat with the emotion of anger.

3) Repugnance and disgust.

4) Parental instinct to protect the young, with tender feeling.

5) Instinctive cry of distress, with feeling of helplessness.

6) Mating or sex instinct with sex emotion.

7) Curiosity, with feeling of wonder.

8) Submission, with feeling of humility.

9) Self-assertion, with feeling of superiority.

10) Seeking company *(herd instinct),* with feeling of loneliness.

11) Food-seeking, with appetite for food.

12) Hoarding instinct, with feeling of ownership.

13) Constructive instinct, with feeling of creativeness.

14) Laughter, with feeling of amusement.

McDougall believes that *"the instincts are not acquired by the individual but handed down to him by heredity. He believes that they play an important role in education."*

Professor E.L. Thorndike of Teachers College of Columbia University, has developed further the theory of education based on instincts further than anyone else. For this reason the classification is given in more detail.

Sensitivity

Children are sensitive to many elements in their environment. All normal children are sensitive to the light waves that enter the eye and stimulate the sense of sight. They are sensitive to a certain range of temperature, to pressure on the skin, to pain, to odor, tastes, and various other elements. The instinct of sensitivity is basic to all life learning.

Attention

Children are so constituted that they instinctively give attention to bright objects, sharp noises, pain, human faces, moving objects, and anything that involves a sharp contrast, like cold after heat.

Gross Bodily Control

The following is a list as bodily activities which are believed to be instinctive: *"Sitting, standing, walking, running, stooping, jumping down, leaping at, crouching, lying down, roll-*

ing over, climbing, dodging, stooping to pick up, raising oneself again, balancing, clinging, pushing with arms and legs, pulling with arms."

Manipulation

The term manipulation designates the instinctive behavior that is sometimes described as construction and destruction. Manipulation of things, whether it is a matter of building or tearing down, is instinctive to every child.

Fear

There is also a group of instincts intimately associated with fear. It is impossible to say that fear is instinctive, because there are as many fears as there are conditions that produce fear. The fear of a snake is not the same as the fear of thunder. It is necessary, then, to list the external forces that are associated with fear.

Thorndike says: "... on the whole it seems likely that an unlearned tendency exists to respond by the physical and mental condition known as fear to the situations, "thunderstorm," "reptiles," "large animals approaching one," "certain vermin," "darkness," and "strange persons of unfriendly mien ..."

Fighting and Anger

There is no specific instinct that leads to fighting, and another that leads to anger. In general it may be said that the situation that leads to anger and fighting in a child most often are those that are connected with instinctive desires that are thwarted.

Eating

Eating is made up of a large number of instinctive acts. The first eating activities of the small baby are instinctive. The seeking of the breasts, the suckling movement of the parts of the mouth, the withdrawal when satisfied and the expulsion of bad tasting material are all unlearned activities of the child. Reaching, grasping, and putting into the mouth form a series of instinctive acts, all which are closely allied with this general activity which we call eating.

Acquisition and Possession

Any object attracts the attention of the child. The appearance of an object, even if it is too large for him to handle will not prevent him, because it awakens his instinctive desire for acquisition and possession of that object. If someone else, particularly another child is already possessing and enjoying the object, the desire for its acquisition and possession becomes much greater. Further more, attempts to keep the object away from the child arouse a dissatisfaction that is satisfied only by acquisition.

Collecting and Hoarding

These instincts are closely related to acquisition and possession. As in the previous discussion, the object must be those that attract attention. They must also be sizable or big enough to carry away and be hoarded.

Hunting

The hunting instinct has always been strong in our ancestors. At first it was a means of food-getting, and became active only when man needed food. At the present time it is not employed as a means of food-getting. We no longer chase game when we are hungry and pounce upon and kill it when we have succeeded in catching it. Even though we do not do this, we still have a great natural joy and satisfaction in catching animals, including men that are fleeing from us.

Habitation

It has been shown that there are a large number of instincts that are grouped in food-getting. In the same manner there are many instincts that are related to habitation. Man, apart from training, responds with discomfort to being shut in a small enclosure, especially if it is a strange one. A child, finding himself in such surroundings, responds by pulling, pushing, kicking and in the case of a child, crying and screaming.

Gregariousness

Children, as well as adults, prefer to be with others of their own kind and are unhappy when alone. Among adults, this desire to live with others, to live in cities, to worship in groups, and to do as many things together as possible.

Attention Getting

In the presence of other human beings who do not frighten one, it seems quite natural to try to attract attention. Human beings do not like to go unnoticed by their fellowmen. This is especially true of children.

Mastery and Submission

These two tendencies have a close relationship with each other. It is instinctive to assert mastery, and also to submit to mastery.

Display and Shyness

These two types of behavior are very closely related to mastery and submission. Display perhaps is, naturally, about the same as mastery, without its crude physical movements. The showing off is a manifestation of the spirit of mastery, over those children or adults for whom the show is given. The result is satisfaction that comes from having someone submit to mastery.

Shyness, with its resultant hesitation, seems to be on the border of submission. The child does not seem to know whether to go to the stranger or run away. In other words he does not know whether to submit to mastery or run away from it.

Rivalry

When a child is engaged in an activity, he naturally does better work if there are other children engaged in the same activity. If he can do the best work, there is a resultant satisfaction. It is probable that any sort of work is done with more interest and better results if it is done in the presence of others, particularly if they are engaged in the same work.

Envy and Jealousy

The actions of envy and jealousy are very closely related to rivalry. In rivalry, the child attempts to do better than another. In envious behavior the child expresses annoyance when he sees another receiving attention or success that he might have had for himself.

Kindliness

The common idea that children are naturally cruel to each other and that have no native goodness as far from being true. It is instinctive to be kind to those in need of help. People who are sick, hungry, or in trouble get sympathy and help from children.

Bullying

The greatest natural tendency that is contrary to kindliness is bullying. It seems to be natural for some children to bully and torment others. The presence of weakness or sickness in another may stimulate the child to kindly behavior, but the presence of other children in competition often produces bullying. This instinct is probably due to a combination of several factors that have been mentioned previously. Teasing is oftentimes closely related to bullying. In fact this type of activity often starts in teasing and develops later into bullying. Whatever the cause or instinctive background it is a very active type of behavior.

Use of Instincts in Education

Professor Clarence E. Ragdale of the University of Wisconsin discusses the various theories concerning instincts, and *concludes:*

"The important question for the parent or teacher is not whether a given kind of behavior is inherited and therefore instinctive, but rather what is the probability that a certain kind of behavior will take place. It is much more important for a first - grade teacher to know the probability of the occurence of such behavior as a fist-fight between two of his pupils than it is to know that such behavior should be labeled instincts or habit ..."

The discussion that follows is based on Ragdale's suggestion which was stated in the preceding topic. Teachers should always learn to work with and not against instinctive tendencies. This is equally true whether the teacher considers instincts to be inborn drives, universal habits, or tendencies.

Thorndike's classification which has been given greatest detail, will be used as the basis for some suggestions as to how original nature maybe worked with in teaching.

Sensitivity is a Basic Instinct

If a child does not have normal receptors, it is impossible for him to learn effectively. Teachers must give attention to the best of care of the sense organs. Many teachers make use of the instinct of attention. It must be remembered, however, that when the child gives attention to a sharp sound the instinctive act is complete. This method does not hold attention. It is much more difficult to hold attention than to get it. Gross Bodily Control shows that if the teacher is to work with natural tendencies, he must give his pupils ample opportunity to do instinctive things that all pupils do. This should mean ample opportunity for physical education and free play.

Manipulation is the instinctive basis for work with the hands. At one time it was common for children to manipulate and destroy school property. In modern school this is unheard of, mostly because the instinctive desire to do things with the hands is satisfied in the school through physical education, industrial arts, and many other subjects.

Fear, Fighting, and Anger should seldom be used in education. They are instincts that should be directed as far as possible into righteous channels.

Collecting and Hoarding often caused misunderstanding between teacher and pupils. The content of the average schoolboy's pocket is evidence of the desire to collect. Sometimes collecting is called stealing when the pupil collects things that belong to another. Children should be directed to make collections that are interesting to them and valuable in their education. It would be possible to go with many more examples of how teachers can work with instincts; but the list above is sufficient to show the necessity of learning about children and how they should be taught.

In general, if instincts are made use of and if the result is satisfying to the child, a habit is formed which will probably last through life. If the activity results from dissatisfaction and will not bring success to the child, the tendency is that this activity will eventually weaken and may soon disappear. If no situation ever arises that calls for the action of an instinct, that instinct will tend to die out through disuse. These, then, are the three main possibilities in the development of activities based on *instincts:*

l) They may be developed into habits.

2) They may die out through resulting dissatisfaction, or

3) They may die out through disuse.

Another possible result is worth mentioning. Substitution of a desired end for an undesired one may be made. If an instinct is leading to bad results, its value may be saved by substituting other situations. A child with a pugnacious instinct may be developing into a troublemaker. The teacher who gives the child a legitimate avenue through which he can exercise the instinct, like basketball or boxing, may save the dynamic power of the natural act without its bad results.

"... it is just a principle of education to utilize individual's original nature as a means of changing him for the better, to produce in him the information, habits, powers, interests, and ideals which are desirable ..."

"The behavior of man in the family, in business, in the state, in religion, and in every other affair of life is rooted in his unlearned, original equipment of instincts and capacities. All schemes of improving life must take account of man's original nature and most of all when their aim is to reverse or counteract it."

Emotions

There are many different points of view concerning emotions. They are considered by various psychologists to be the following possibilities; instinctive reactions, results of bodily activities, conscious product of the brain and nervous system, and results of mental confusion.

1) Emotions as instincts. Whose classification of instincts was discussed earlier in this chapter, holds to the instinctiveness of emotions. He had made a list of instincts with their accompanying emotions. The instincts of escapes, or self-preservation, are accompanied by the emotions of fear, terror, and fright. Combat is accompanied by tender emotion, and love. Assertion and self-display are accompanied by elation and feeling of superiority.

2) Emotions as the result of bodily activities. In 1884, William James, American psychologist, and Carl Lange, a Danish physician, independently announced a theory of emotions. Since that time this theory has been known as the James Lange theory of emotions. Briefly, it holds that the other theorty of events leading up to emotions *is:*

a) an exciting stimulus

b) conscious recognition

c) bodily activities

d) the emotion

A child sees a certain dog, recognizes it as an enemy, runs, and is afraid. ***Emotion is the ultimate result of activity.*** It may be activity of the muscles or activity in the internal organs, The James-Lange theory has had many followers among psychologists, and many have attacked it. Dr. John B. Watson and his followers deny the existence of instincts, and consider emotions to be *"profound changes of the bodily mechanism as a whole, but particularly of the visceral and glandular system."* This can be considered a modified form of the James-Lange theory.

Other Theories Concerning Emotions

One school of psychology believes emotions to be instinctive, but that would reduce the number of original emotions to sex, or sex and ego. All other emotions are explained in terms of these two. Though this school has many followers, it has been criticized as one-sided and unsatisfactory. Finally, there are those who believe that emotions are the conscious product of the brain and the nervous system.

Emotions and Education

Emotions exist and are ever present in school children. It matters little what theory of emotions is believed by the teacher if he knows their educational implications.

Functions of Health: It is important to know that emotions are closely related to health. Excitement makes the heart beat rapidly. Sadness interrupts the direction. In fact, continued emotions of any kind help to disrupt the visceral organs. It is well known that continued emotions of worry, anxiety, and sadness prevent the body from normal functioning and delay recovery from illness. This must not be taken to mean that all emotions are bad. They are not. Such emotions as joy and happiness are good for the body. Physical exercise done for fun of it is of more value to the body than the same exercise undergone through compulsion. This explains the present-day tendency to make all physical training in the school such as games and free play. A teacher should remember that schoolroom in which there is a spirit of joy is better for the health of children than one in which fear, sadness and worry emanates.

Emotions and Learning

When a teacher wishes to teach children to read, write, spell or fix number combinations, he must deal carefully with emotions. The joy of doing well and the desire to do the best work in the room are examples of positive emotions, that is, emotions that are helpful. But the teacher must guard against fear, dread, and worry, because they interfere with the normal process of learning. Fright may completely stop the learning process and prevent the child from doing his best. Anger, nervousness, chagrin, anxiety, worry, fear, and all such emotions should be kept out of the classroom as much as possible. The teacher should learn the fine art of controlling emotional responses.

Emotions and Appreciation

We know much more about training the muscles and developing the intellect than we do about emotions. The old school with its reading, writing, and arithmetic had no use for emotions. When physical education, health, history, and other subjects were added to the curriculum, there was little education that affected the emotional life. But the modem curriculum with its art, music, literature, and citizenship has a vast emotional appeal. Art is taught in the modern school to develop the love of artistic things. This does not mean just pictures, but dress, house, decorations, and everything with which the pupil comes in contact. The aim of such education is to develop the love for artistry that will last through life. In the same way children learn to appreciate good music. If the school is able to develop in children a lasting love for the good and beautiful, then it has done its part in nurturing the education of the emotions.

THE TEACHER AND THE
LEARNING PROCESS

A teacher must know what learning is. He must know how children learn, what makes them learn and what makes them fail to learn. He must also know what are the most favorable conditions to maximum learning. There can be no teaching without the learner, although there may be learning without a teacher. The child is therefore, the *"raison d'etre" (see page 39)* of teaching. And learning is the purpose of all teaching. But what is learning?

Learning

Learning *"is both a process and a product."* The child's endeavor to learn is the process and once the things are learned it becomes a product. The product of learning may be good or bad depending upon whether or not it serves a useful purpose. And the purpose of teaching is to serve as the guidance of learning something socially useful and desirable.

The Nature of Learning

According to Klausmeier, learning is a mental process by which people adjust to their environment in an intelligent rational way. It includes organizing and valuable experiences into more meaningful patterns of understanding an action. It is more efficient if it is purposeful. However, we often learn incidentally by giving close attention to things in our environment.

Factors in the Learning Process

There are four factors in the teaching-learning process, namely: *"the child, the teacher, the setting, and the purpose."*

1) The Child - The child is a thinking, living organism. He is endowed by nature with the capabilities of learning and development. He has inherited certain drive, instincts, and reflexes, as well as physical and mental capabilities that enable him to learn.

2) The Teacher - The teacher more than any body else is in a position to help the child learn. He is, like the child, a part of the teaching-learning process. He helps select the situation, provides the motivation and determines the kind of experiences children should learn in any given time.

3) The Setting - The school environment influences to a large degree the kind and extent of progress in learning the child could attain. The school must be a pleasant and happy place to live in. It must be a home to all children. It must provide children with the right conditions for growth.

4) The Purpose - The aims and objectives of learning must be understood by both the child and the teacher. Purpose must be clear and must be within the level of understanding of children. It should be achievable.

Purposeful Learning

Learning follows a developmental pattern. At a given stage of maturation, an individual is motivated to satisfy a biological or social need that creates tension in him. To satisfy the need and to relieve tension he strives to reach a goal which he aims with proper motivation. There are five essential features of purposeful learning *namely:*

1) The individual is motivated.

2) He directs attention toward the goal and expends energy directed to it.

3) He engages in trial-and-error activity to find a new method.

4) He applies previous experience to the task.

5) In the process of differentiation and integration, he

drops inappropriate methods, confirms the correct ones, and incorporates the new method into learned behavior patterns.

Conditions that Affect Progress in Learning

1) Readiness for learning which *includes:*

    a) mental motivation

    b) physical motivation

    c) experimental background

2) Intelligence

    a) mechanical intelligence

    b) abstract intelligence

    c) social intelligence

3) Intensity of Motivation

    a) rewards and punishments

    b) feeling of success or failure

    c) knowledge of progress

4) Already Learned Work Methods

5) Social and Emotional Adjustments

6) Health and Physical Fitness

Principles Underlying the Learning Process

1) People learn best when they are actively working to grasp opportunities to solve problems.

2) Interest stimulates and aids learning.

3) Learning of any kind depends upon readiness which is compounded by attitude, physical skills, physical growth, and interest. We often think of readiness in terms of maturity, but it is a matter of experience and growth rather than of age.

4) Total organism is involved in learning. Together an individual's brain, nerves, muscles, and emotions, respond to all experiences.

5) Learning involves the reconstruction and recognition of experience. It adds to the meaning of experience and increases the ability to direct the cause of subsequent events.

6) Learning is the process of acquiring new responses or adjustments and is evidenced by changes in behavior.

7) When an organism faces a novel situation, old responses will not suffice. A new response is called for or failure confronts it. If fortunately the organism

contrives a new response it is what we call learning.

8) Organizing the teaching - learning situation effectively calls for the *following:*

    a) Fulfill the interests and needs of children.

    b) Make instruction meaningful.

    c) Use instructional materials.

9) Practice procedures should be:

    a) Intensive, vigorous, motivated, and distributed over a length of time.

    b) By wholes or parts of wholes.

    c) Guides

Other Principles of Learning

1) Learning is more efficient when it is related to pupil purpose.

2) Growth and learning are continuous.

3) Each child is unique in his rate of learning.

4) Children learn several things at once. They do not learn one thing at a time. This is known as the principle of concomittant learnings. Incidental learnings to the main task is frequently as important as the material to

be learned.

5) A child learns best when the task is adjusted to his level.

6) Children learn best through life-like experiences.

Knowledge and Learning

The problem in the classroom is not the accumulation of facts, but one that is helping the pupils to translate the knowledge gained so that it becomes meaningful to his experience. It is the process of learning and not the answering of questions which constitute the core of education. Learning occurs when the entire personality of the pupil is involved. Knowledge which is meaningful is not merely cerebral. Genuine knowledge involves the viscera, the muscles, and the glands. The teacher's concern however is not how much the pupil knows and how well he learns. The pupil, not the book, nor the examination, should be the problem of the teacher.

Kinds of Learning Recognized Today

1) Learning basic intellectual skills. Ability to read, listen, speak, write, and the use of mathematics which are essential to normal and effective living.

2) Learning motor skills. Walking, dancing using a hammer, laying a brick, removing or expanding, *etc.*

3) Learning to adjust to new situations. Encountering new, unforeseen situations is a normal experience for everyone.

4) Learning social skills. Abilities, habits, skills, attribute needs to work and play with others.

5) Learning to be creative. Ability to speak, write, sing, paint and dance in ways which give pleasure or convey new ideas. It includes the development of all of the child's powers of imagination and self-expression.

Forms of Learning
According to Beauchamp

1) *Motor learning* - There are two parts in motor learning, the sensory-motor learning and the perceptual-motor

learning. Motor activities are further grouped into three *categories:*

a) Object-motor

b) Language-motor

c) Feeling-motor activities

A) *Object Motor Activities* - refer to those involved in the attainment or the manipulation of physical objects.

B) *Object Language Motor Activities* - refer to all activi- ties embracing the use of the speech organs, the eyes, as in reading process and in the hand-and-arm muscles.

C) *Feeling Motor Activities* - are exemplified in such activities as the dance, vocal music, the playing of instrument, *etc.*

2) *Mental associations* - Mental association takes place in various forms. It may be relating of two different concepts to a general concept or a matter of learning the same response to two different stimuli.

3) *Conditioning* - This is a matter of substituting a new response for a familiar stimuli. Example: *"a scalded dog is afraid of cold water."*

4) *Trial-and-error learning* - It may either be motor-

learning or mental association. I call it response or varied reaction.

Four Factors
Fundamental to Learning

1) Drive - or motivation is caused by tension resulting from a felt need and arousing the organism to seek satisfaction of this need.

2) Cue - is the stimulus or combination of stimuli that determines when and where the individual will react and the kind of response that will be made.

3) Response - is the act or thought - what a person does to relieve the tension caused by the felt need.

4) Reward - satisfaction of felt need which results in a reinforcement that strengthens the tendency for a response to be repeated.

The Higher Mental Processes

These include conceptualization, generalization, reasoning, and thinking.

1) **Conceptualizaion** is the process of abstraction and integration.

2) **Generalization** is the process of organizing a group of specific facts of information into a form that is non-specific but applicable to a number of specific kinds of situations.

3) **Reasoning** - is the process by which an individual reaches his goals because he is able to form relationships that he has never made before. Reasoning defines as *"the ability to combine the essentials of two isolated experiences in such a manner as to reach a goal."*

4) **Thinking** - is the most complex of the higher mental processes. Thinking utilizes the symbolism of language and other abstractions from conceptualization so as to create something new or something different.

5) **Problem solving** - is the process of resolving a difficulty by the use of known principles of induction and deduction.

GENERALIZATIONS RELATING TO THE EDUCATIVE PROCESS

1) Learning and behavior are caused - The stature to which a person can grow and develop is determined by heredity but the kind of person he will be is determined largely by his environment.

2) The organism acts as a whole - Making an oral response to a sarcastic remark involves not only the mind and vocal chords but also the emotions.

3) The child and his environment are inseparable entities. A person's behavior does not take place in a vacuum. He is always behaving or reacting in relation to persons, objects, or situations.

4) Learning takes place in problem solving - All learning involves the solving of problems.

5) Learning implies activity - All kinds of learning involve some kind of activity, mental, or physical.

6) Creativity - is an essential aspect of all learning. All kinds of learning involve some amount of newness or a rearrangement of aspects of old situations to form new ones.

7) The individual must be motivated to learn. Motivation arises out of a child's desire to meet needs.

8) Learning is largely an emotional experience.

9) To learn is to change. Minimally however, learning does not occur unless what is learned can be put to use. Learning has many dimensions - reasoning, feeling, acting, expressing, and evaluating.

PROPOSITIONS
OF MODERN LEARNING

1) A pupil learns only what he is interested in learning. The focus of interest is the chief determinant in the quality of pupil performance.

2) It is important that pupils share in the development of the curriculum.

3) Learning is integral. Learning is not additive experience but a remaking of experience.

4) Learning depends upon wanting to learn.

5) An individual learns best when he is free to create his

own response in a situation. His present experience is the only experience he undergoes.

6) Learning depends upon not knowing the answers. Knowing the answer without recognizing the problems blocks understanding and discovery.

7) Every pupil learns his own way. A teacher wants a pupil to learn his own way instead of the child's own way. Every pupil is different. There is no living *"average"* pupil. An average is a quantitative, mathematical, abstract, concept.

FOUR FUNDAMENTALS
OF LEARNING PROCESS

1)   The child must want something *(drive or motive)*

2)   The child must notice something *(cue)*

3)   The child must do something *(response)*

4)   The child must got something *(reward)*

THE LAWS OF LEARNING

Nothing *"just happens."* Everything that takes place in life is the result of a cause, and the same cause with the same set of circumstances produces a result. Learning, whether it is the learning of an animal or human being, follows this general rule. An animal trainer, in order to be successful in his work, must understand how animals learn. If he works in violation of known cause-result relationships, he finds it impossible to accomplish his purpose. The reason most of us cannot teach an animal to do circus tricks is that we do not understand the general principle of animal learning. It is necessary to know the effect of punishment, food, kind words, and other factors, in order to teach an animal. In the same manner it is necessary to know the basic laws of child learning in order to be *"successful in teaching"* a child. Many of us attended school whose teachers had no knowledge of the learning process. As a result we have many bad intellectual habits and many deficiencies that skillful teachers would have prevented.

The Brain and the Nervous System

In order to understand how children learn, it is necessary to know something about the brain and the nervous system. There is a close relationship between the learning process and the activity of the brain and the nervous system.

The brain and nervous system are made up of nerve cells that are called neurons. These cells are long fibers and can be seen only with the aid of a microscope. A cross section of a nerve will show that it is made up of many fibers very much like that of a telephone cable is made up of a large number of separate wires. The brain is made up of millions of these neurons. To carry the telephone analogy a step further, the brain is analogous to *"central."* The nerves carry the messages to and from the brain, and make the necessary connections. Like when you see a coin and pick it up. This act started when a nerve carried the message from the eye to the brain. The brain made the necessary connection and the hand reached for the coin. Of course this is a simple explanation. When you study Educational Psychology, much more will be learned about the brain and the nervous system.

Neurons has three important properties: (1) *sensitivity*. (2) *conductivity*, and (3) *modifiability*.

By *sensitivity* means that neurons are sensitive to certain elements in their environment. This sensitivity is made possible because of the receptors. The eye is a simple example. It is a sense organ or the receptor. Neurons ending in the retina of the eye are sensitive to the either waves that cause the individual to have the sensation of light. On the other hand, neurons that have their endings in the inner ear are sensitive to certain air waves that are known to us as sound. In a similar manner all of the nerve endings in the receptors are sensitive to certain stimuli.

By *conductivity* means that neurons are capable of transmitting impulses from one part of the nervous system to another. When the sensitive nerve endings in the retina of the eye are stimulated, the neurons transmit this impulse to the brain and the sensation of light results. We hear sounds because neurones ending in the ear are sensitive to sound waves, and the impulse set up is conducted to the brain. A man sees that a fence is about to fall down and steps back to avoid being hurt. From the standpoint of this discussion it is possible to say that the neurons that end in the eye were stimulated and the optic nerve transmitted the message to the brain. At this point the man comprehended the situation and another impulse traveled to the neurons ending in the muscles; the result was that the man moved.

By *modifiability* means that the neurons are subject to modification. Connections or tendencies to connect between neurones are a part of man's equipment when he comes into the world. They account for, in part, the inborn tendencies. When you enter a bright room coming from a dark room, the pupils of your eyes constrict. This is unlearned and common to the race. The child comes into the world with such neuron connections that the stimulation of bright light brings about the contraction of the muscles which contol the size of the pupils. When a child first sees something bright, he reaches for it. This is an example of a tendency to connect between neurons. If however, the act results in dissatisfaction to the child, the next time he sees a bright light he may not reach for it. In other words, the original tendency to connection may be modified. This modifiability of neurons is fundamental to the learning process. We cannot say that a person have learned anything unless the process of learning has modified his neurons.

All learning is based upon these three properties of neurons. Nothing new can be learned without sensitivity; no impulse can reach the brain without the necessary conductivity; and no learning based upon experience is possible without modifiability.

The explanation given above for the learning process is very simple, but is essentially used by many psychologists. It offers the simplest and most satisfactory basis upon which to explain the laws of learning.

Important Laws of Learning

The law of learning that follows is considered the most important for the teacher to know and use. Different psychologists employ different names for these laws. The names used in this outline are those that are most common.

It should be noted in the beginning that these laws are operative only when the child has the normal receptors, a functioning nervous system, and enough native ability to be able to learn.

Much has been written about *"hit or miss"* or *"trial and error"* learning. The assumption is that when a child meets a situation he does something. That something may be right or wrong. The important thing for learning is that he does something. A hungry cat in a pen with food in sight will do many things. A child with a new toy which is not familiar to him may do many things with that toy. It is also important that a child does something when he meets a learning situation. It is also important that the teacher knows what to do in order to aid the learning process. The following laws are given for the teacher to use so that learning may be directed instead of *"hit or miss."*

The law of effect. A child tends to do over again a thing that has resulted in or has been accompanied by satisfaction. On the other hand he tends to avoid and fails to repeat those reactions that are annoying.

This law is fundamental to learning. Its working is made possible through the modifiability of the neurons. A child puts a stick of candy into his mouth and the result is satisfying. Very soon this child is putting everything that looks like candy into his mouth. If a child sees a cat, pulls its tail and gets scratched, he will tend not to do it again. If he does try it again with the same annoying result he is certain to discontinue this particular activity.

Satisfiers and *annoyers* are great educators. This law seems to be so reasonable and so common that anyone would be aware of it even if he had not studied psychology. However, a review of the teachings in the past shows that teachers have almost entirely ignored it. If a teacher took advantage of the law of effect, he would see to it that effective work and satisfying situations were connected. Yet the opposite has been too often true. It has been common practice in the past for teachers to keep children after school as a punishment. The teacher who does this ignores the law of effect, because he has deliberately made school work an annoyer. It would be much more sensible to send the bad boy home early, and give the good child privilege of remaining in school until the end of the day. This has been very successfully tried in many modern schools. If you wish children to love school, the school work must always be a joy and never used as a punishment. The teacher who makes a boy learn poety as a punishment for being bad also violates the law of effect. The school should not teach boys and girls to love good poetry. When poetry is used as a punishment and they were made to memorize verses upon verses, it becomes an *"annoyer"* to the pupil, and often completely kills his enjoyment of poetry. The school should not force boys and girls to love poetry if they do not want to.

The connection of satisfaction and good situations does not mean that the teacher should give prizes for good work. The natural results of a well-done piece of work should be satisfying, and the situation should be so arranged that the natural results of a poor piece of work should be annoying.

The Law of Use. It was once said that, *"whenever a modifiable connection between a situation and a response is experienced, other things being equal, the strength of that* *connection is increased."* In other words, the often a child does a certain situation, the more likely he is to make the same response in the future. The doing of a thing many times tends to make it a permanent habit. If a child spelled *"until"* with two "1's" for a hundred times, it would be very unlikely to get him to spell the word as it should be spelled. If a child is always made to think of 4 when he sees 2x2, this will soon be a permanent connection.

The converse of this law is often called the law of disuse. By disuse we mean that when a *"situation-response"* connection is not used, the tendency is for the connection to weaken and fall away. *For example,* a child may learn to spell a word correctly. Though frequent practice of the spelling or frequent usage of the word, he may spell it correctly at first. However, as months pass by, the connections that were made may weaken especially if has not used the word further. He will find it necessary to learn to spell the word again. In this connection we should mention another law of learning that is closely connected with disuse, that is, the law of regency. Other things being equal, the more recent the exercise the stronger the connection between situation and response.

These are basic in teaching. When an arithmetic combination was learned once, it must be recalled at frequent intervals in order to keep the connection intact. The same thing is true of everything that is learned by repetition.

The law of use, regency, and effect are the bases of all drill works in the schools. Three things are necessary in any good drill *lesson:* (1) **the correct connection must be made**, (2) **the connection must be repeated,** and (3) **the correct connection should result in satisfaction of the child**. If you wish children to learn all of the multiplication and addition combinations, it may be necessary to present these combinations many times and have them correctly repeated or written by the child, and the result to the child must be satisfying. Practice in correct writing is another example of the law of exercise, the vital point being that the correct connection should always be made.

The law of readiness. The principle or law of readiness is as *follows:* The more an individual is ready to act in a certain way, the satisfying it will be for him to act in that way and the more frustrating it will be not to act in that way. Conversely, the more unready an individual is to act in a certain way, the more annoying or awful it will be for him to act in that way.

Teachers should work with and not against readiness. This is very important, particularly with young children. Readiness is closely related with the law of effect. If children are in a state of readiness for an exercise, the result is more likely to be satisfying, and it is more apt to be done all over again. Enthusiasm for work, motivation, and joy in attacking a task are all part of readiness.

The Law of Mind Set. The response that a child gives to any situation depends upon the general set of that child's mind. This law is also related to readiness. A certain stimulus does not always produce the same response in the same person. Ask a little girl this question, *"Do you like to play?"* The response will vary depending upon the condition or general mind set of the child at the time the question was asked. If she is at the piano, she may decline that offer but if she is playing with her dolls, she may reply otherwise. In a magazine article, there was a discussion about a group of students which shows another example of mind-set was found. The article concerning the greatest men of America was written by James Havey Robinson. Dewey was named as one of the group. When this name was given, some members of the group thought of Admiral Dewey, and others of John Dewey, the philosopher. The difference was a mind set.

There are several laws that are closely related to the general principle of mind set. *Law of Relativity* is one of them. According to this law any stimulus will be interpreted not by itself alone, but in its relationship to other stimuli that may accompany or precede it. Sour after sweet is not the same as sour after peppery. A merchant in selling damaged goods after a fire made use of this law by displaying the blackened goods on a black background. If displayed on a white background they would have looked much more soiled. *The Law of Diminishing Returns* is another *law* that is related to the principle of mind set. A stimulus will produce a more intense result only when a weak stimulus is added rather than a strong one. Hence, an ounce added to a pound may not be noticed, but an ounce added to an ounce is noticed at once. A short line added to a long line will not be perceived but if a long line is added to a short line, it is immediately seen.

Teachers who do not know these laws often misinterpret children. Confusion takes place especially when a teacher, having only one set of mind, asked a question and the child answered differently. Mind set also explains in part why some children find it difficult to understand a certain question while others do not. It also explains the misinterpretation of examination questions. Teachers must also be familiar with relativity and diminishing returns in order to make the situation be the best stimulus for the children. The order and manner in which material presented should always be determined on the basis of these laws.

The law of analogy. When a child meets a new situation and has no special instincts or habits to determine the response, he responds as he has responded in the past to a like situation. This is the law of analogy.

The servant who threw water on Sir Walter Raleigh when he saw him smoking was reasoning by analogy. For the servant, he perceived the smoke he saw while person's clothing was on fire which happened in the past as the same situation as what he saw while Sir Walter was smoking. Hence the water was thrown to put the fire out. Another situation was the man who drank from his finger bowl. He was seated in a dinner table and a bowl of water was placed before him. In his past experience water before him at a dinner table meant something to drink. So he drank. A young child who has eaten colored sticks of candy may put a colored stickor even a striped worm into his mouth.

In all the foregoing cases a new situation has been met by response based upon a like situation. In all of these situations the solution has been faulty. In school work correct analogies are common, and much value may be obtained through their use. A child may be led to pronounce correctly a new work through its relationship to a known word. If a child can pronounce *"cat"* he may, through the relationship, correctly pronounce *"mat."* Furthermore, he may often get the correct meaning of a new word through its relationship to one or more known words. Many arithmetic problems may be solved correctly by relating them to known methods of solution. In geography the occupations of certain people may be distinguished through the relationship of their country to another.

Teachers should make constant use of this type of learning. Many new situations may be solved by the children when the teacher takes the time to point out analogies. Children should be taught that solutions of this kind are an aid to learning, but that the solutions should be carefully verified.

The Law of Analysis. It has been said, *"that it thus seems to be general law of mind that any element of mental life which is* *felt as a part of many total mental states differing in all else save its presence comes thereby to be belt as an idea by itself."*

Learning through analysis is a higher type of learning than any other just referred to. When we are making use of the laws of use and effect we are learning directly through simple associations. In analysis we have much more complicated learning. If we wish to teach a child the meaning of the word *"perpendicular,"* we may not do it by analysis. If a child is shown some perpendicular object, through association he may think that the word perpendicular refers to the object rather than the position of the object. In order to overcome this difficulty we teach a concept of perpendicular through analysis.

By using examples like a perpendicular wall, a pencil held in a perpendicular position, a string with a weight fastened on it, and in many other situations depicting the perpendicular element, we may get the child to understand what we mean by perpendicular. When these different situations are presented to the child, it is necessary for him to compare them and to see that they are alike in one particular aspect of being perpendicular. When he sees this likeness through all of them, the teacher should supply the new term, which is the word *"perpendicular."* All ideas such as these should be taught through a process of analysis.

Furthermore, many subjects can be better taught by analysis than by the common means of association. An example of this is teaching the pronunciation of short *"e."* A teacher may mark short *"e,"* pronounce it for the child and have it pronounced several times; thus the child learns it through the law of use. However, it makes for much greater independence in the child if the sound is taught through analysis. The child is already familiar with a large number of words containing the short *"e."* If these words are placed on the blackboard and the child notices that they differ in all else save the pressence of an *"e"* that is sounded in the same way, it will be possible for him to abstract from all these situations this single element which will be the correct sound for short *"e."* If he is taught to pronounce in this manner, it will be much easier for him to handle such situations independently later on.

Probably the best example of teaching through analysis is teaching the meaning of numbers. Take for example the teaching of the meaning of the number *"4."* A child probably learns first of all the word *"four"* in connection with the counting of his fingers. Most parents teach children to count in this manner. If he begins counting with his little finger, then *"four"* becomes the name of the fourth finger. There is no idea of number in this. A child probably will pass from this stage to the counting stage where he starts from one and counts to a hundred. He may still have no number sense. Four here will mean that word which comes between three and five in a list of associations. When such a child starts to count and is stopped, it is necessary for him to start again in order to get his association straight. The word *"four"* may be written on the board, or the figure *"4"* maybe placed on the board and the child is told that this is *"four."* However, he may even recognize the word and the symbol without having any idea of what is meant by four.

To teach the *"fourness"* of this number it is necessary to teach it through analysis. If a child is presented with four chalk marks on the board, four pencils, four windows on the side of the room, four classmates and four sounds produced by tapping, and is asked to find the common element, he will probably for the first time get the *"fourness"* of four. This is a case where a child has come in contact with a large number of total situations differing in all else save the presence of a common element. He tends to feel this common element as an idea by itself.

This description of the law of analysis does not mean to imply that all learning is analytical. We cannot explain learning exclusively in terms of analysis. Learning is also synthetic or constructive. In developing the meaning of *"fourness"* we have constructed something new, a new form of response. The important task in teaching is the construction of something that is new to the learner. This is the result of a process we call thinking. The cultivation of thinking as a creative process or as a reconstruction of old habits is of fundamental importance.

The laws which have been given in this outline are the most common laws of learning. A teacher who masters and makes use of them will do much better teaching than one who is ignorant of their existence. It is well to remember that all learning takes place in accordance with the laws.

THE CURRICULUM

Nature of Curriculum

Teaching according to someone is a matter of knowing where you want to go and of having the means of going there. Knowing where to go is the purpose and aim of education and the means of going there is the curriculum.

(1) The curriculum represents the total life of the school. In its widest sense, the curriculum refers to all the experiences and activities engaged in by children under the direction of the school.

Part of the curriculum are:

a) working

b) studying

c) playing

d) including the materials used

e) the methods followed

f) the goals set to be realized.

A limited meaning of curriculum would refer it to a body of subjects or courses offered in a school, college, or university as a prerequisite to graduation in a specific course, as the elementary, secondary, agricultural, or trade school curriculum.

(2) The curriculum is something to be experienced rather than something to be learned. Education is a continuous process. It never ends. It is never completed. The curriculum as a tool in the educative process, therefore, has a vital function in the life of every one even long after the child has left school. The curriculum is experienced. It is vital, it is alive. Book learning is not all unless what has been learned in them is translated into experiences.

(3) The child is more important than the subject matter. We teach children, not subject matter. The child deserves sympathy, consideration, understanding. The subject matter does not deserve sympathy although it must be understood in order to be experienced.

(4) The subject matter is a means to an end; the end being the wholesome development of the pupil being served. The subject has no reason to exist without the learner to give meaning to it. The wholesome development of the child is the end. It is therefore fallacious to fail a child because he could not profit and make use of it. To do so would be to make the subject matter the end instead of the means to an end.

(5) In educational planning, there can be no progress without change, although there may be change without progress. The development of the curriculum is a continuous process; and in order to develop there must be changes for the better. But changes alone do not mean progress. Changes may only be in form but not in substance.

(6) The improvement of the school program should begin where the teacher is just as learning in the classroom must begin where the pupil is. The school program cannot be improved unless the teacher has the knowledge and the skill and the readiness to effect the desired change. It is useless to demand that all teachers use the newer techniques if they do not know what they are, how they are to be done, and the theories and principles underlying them.

(7) Teachers should realize that they do have more freedom in determining what they teach and on how to teach it. While there are sources to be looked into and objectives suggested for achievement, yet the teacher have plenty of freedom to modify or even reject them as he sees fit considering the peculiarities of his own children. However, he must have a tenable reason for his choice.

(8) The school program is not static. It is flexible. It goes either forward or backward. In order to provide for individual differences in both pupils and teachers the school progam cannot be fixed and made rigidly inflexible.

---

*Tips on ... "**Love and Kindness**" are two of the sweetest and happiest words in the world. They are the sugar of life, making the bitter sweet, and the rough smooth. Just as syrup soothes a sore throat, so does kindness heal the unhappiness of the heart."*

"Love and kindness also give us the great gift of friendship, with all the happiness which goes with it. Friendship teaches us loyalty; surely friendship without loyalty is false and empty. And we learn, last of all, that the expression of kindness and friendship is generosity."

"So let us plant love and kindness, friendship and generosity in our hearts, and help them to grow and blossom, so that by our service they may bear the precious fruit of happiness."

Curriculum Resources for Teaching and Learning

The exclusive use of textbooks in the classroom is gone. Present trends in teaching calls for the use of a wide variety of means and media for teaching and learning. While textbooks are still in use, they are supplemented by various means such as the *following:*

(1) *Community resources*. The great big book of nature has resources that are inexhaustible. The child is to help in realizing that learning can be had from the things in his environment. The community around him - the people, their various activities and institutions, *etc.,* could provide challenges that should evoke learning.

There are two kinds of resources in the community.

a)   *Material resources* - such as markets, roads, bridges, mines and minerals, forests, seas, plants and animals, factories and industries, *etc.*

b)   *Human resources* - Refers to people in the community - the local talent, the professional, the farmer, industrialist, businessman, parent, priest or minister, and so on.

To be able to make use of these resources, the teacher has the following media:

a) *Field trips* - Field trips should not be confused with an excursion. A field trip is well planned. It has a distinct educational purpose. An excursion has for its primary aim recreation and enjoyment although it may have realized an educational purpose. In a field trip, children are guided what to see, observe, gather materials to report and so on.

b) *Interviews* - By pupils with local officials, parents, industrial managers, farmers, and local leaders in politics, and industry.

c) *Resource persons* - Local talents who have the experience and training in specific areas of knowledge and invited to share his experiences with pupils.

d) *Service centers* - The Red Cross, Chest Clinic, Hospital, Puericulture Centers, Maternity Clinic, Prison, Provincial Museum and Demonstration Centers - these are availed of to obtain certain information that could be profitably used in the classroom or to enrich the curriculum.

e) ***Service projects*** - Pupils may help and talk about such activities as the anti-littering campaign. Clean-up weekends with people in the community for a pay either by the hour, by piecemeal jobs, or by daily wages.

f) ***Work experience*** - Pupils and students may work during weekends with people in the community. Students and big pupils may not only earn pocket money but actually gain experience. Work hours for students in secondary schools and colleges are wasted every year in some country due to lack of opportunity for their profitable use.

g) ***Camping*** - This is a relatively new practice in the field of education. Schools take their pupils to a selected camp-site and camp there for a few days to a week's time. Experiences in democratic planning, cooperative living, self-reliance, health and safety, etc., are made parts of the program.

(2) ***Creative Resources***. The second group of resources from which the teacher could draw upon to provide learning experiences to his children may be classified as creative resources. Construction work, music and art, drawing, dramatic play, readings and projects in literature are varied means of learning that should challenge the pupils' imagination. Creative experien-

ces provide opportunities for self-expression, appreciation, and understanding.

(3) **Socializing Resources.** Present trends in education give stress to group planning and other cooperatively run socialized forms of endeavor. There is no limit to which a class can do to provide for an opportunity for group planning and action. The class may set up cooperatively planned program, committee reports and activities, or may set up pupil clubs and organizations, publish newspapers, etc., where mutual consultations and group deliberations are in evident.

(4) *Audio-Visual Resources*. Many teachers mistake Audio-Visual resources to mean only films and film-strips projected on a screen which can be no farther from the truth. Audio-Visual resources include all pupil-made posters, drawings, mounted and unmounted, graphs, diagrams, dioramas, etc. Teaching devices like the felt-board and electric board could be used to hold cut-outs, word-cards, pictures, etc., that could vitalize the lesson. Real objects, mounted objects, collections of shells, insects, flowers, rocks, etc., in a museum are all Audio-Visual materials. Maps, radios, phonographs, etc., are no longer rare in the classroom today as they were a few years ago.

(5) **Reading Resources**. Reading resources include all kinds of reading matter as textbooks, supplementary readers, reference books, encyclopedias, home reading books, resource books, etc., periodicals such as magazines, newspapers, newsletters, bulletins; Bureau of Public School publications such as circulars, memorandums, bulletins, circular letters, brochures, monographs; statistical abstracts; reports of national and local committees on education, and so on, belong to this category. Reading activities are not confined to textbooks alone but to as many sources as can be had by the teacher. A class may use books one or two grades above or below its grade level if in the opinion of the teacher there is a need of it.

Developing and Organizing
the Curriculum

As we pointed out, the curriculum refers to all activities engaged in by the children under the direction of the school. These activities however must be so organized that they can be made use of by both teacher and his pupils. There are several factors that should be considered in the development and organization of the curriculum.

(1) *Philosophy of Education*. This refers to our beliefs and concepts of what the nature and purposes of education our children need. What do we want our children to learn? Why do we want our children to learn them? What aspects of our culture must we want our children to master? why?

(2) *Principles and Psychology of Education*. Learning, to be useful, must be meaningful. It must reflect life outside of school. It should be suited to the child's level of maturity and should be learned through effort or self-activity.

(3) *Basic needs and Interests of Children*. Things to be learned should be those that meet the immediate needs of children, those that help to develop their sense of personal worth

and integrity.

(4) *Nature of Society*. What we want our children to learn must partly spring from our culture and social heritage. It should reflect our society's political, economic, and social concerns.

Principles of Curriculum Development

The development of the curriculum is governed by certain principles among which are mentioned the following:

(1) *The Curriculum should be comprehensive*. It is all-embracing. It must include aspects of human life - its needs, its hopes and desires, its trials and tribulations.

(2) *It must be a product of cooperative endeavor*. The curriculum should be the result of cooperative thinking of all - teachers, pupils, school administrators and supervisors, parents, laymen, social and civic leaders in the community, and so on.

(3) *It must be Articulated*. The curriculum should be so made that children progress from one grade to another conti-nuously.

(4) *It should be continuous*. Curriculum building is a continuous process. It changes as the needs of the people change.

(5) *It should be concrete*. The curriculum is based on a concrete foundation. Nothing goes into the curriculum unless it reflects the present and future demands of society.

(6) *It must be flexible*. It should allow for individual and group differences. It should be so constructed that modifications could be introduced without destroying its use.

(7) *It must be determined by those who will use it*. To be functional, it must reflect the needs of the children for whom it is built.

(8) *It should reflect the social organization of the community*. While individual needs and group needs may differ yet both have many things in common. The curriculum should provide for both.

Approaches to the Selection
of Curriculum Content

The main criterion for the selection of the curriculum content is *"social usage."* This means nothing is put into the curriculum that has no use in actual life. The child, his activities, needs, and interests become the dominating criterion relative to the curriculum.

Whatever are selected, they are supposed to lead towards the development of an integrated individual. In curriculum work, integration has three *meanings:*

(1) a well balanced individual *(physiological integration)*

(2) a well organized functional social unit *(social integration)* and

(3) unified learning experiences having meaning for the individual.

There are several ways by which the content of the curriculum could be selected *namely:*

(1) *The textbook approach*. This is the oldest way and is no longer in exclusive use. While textbooks are still used they are no longer looked upon as the only source of what is to be

taught in a given situation.

(2) *The course of study approach*. There are still courses of study being issued to the field from the General Office. Like the textbook the course of study is to be supplemented with other sources like information gathered from newspapers, magazines, bulletins, guides, manuals, statistical data, and so on.

(3) *The objective approach*. The National Committee on Education has formulated objectives for implementation in the field. These objectives are broken down into smaller immediate objectives which could serve as the basis for the selection of materials and activities in the classroom.

(4) *The center of interest approach*. It is held that children at different ages, grades, or experience levels, have different tastes and interests. Subject matter is selected on the basis of changing interests.

(5) *The child-centered approach*. Oftentimes the curriculum is selected on the basis of a hypothetical individual child whose interests and needs had been analyzed and made the basis of the selections.

(6) *The community-centered approach*. This refers to the selection of subject matter used on the conditions, needs, and

interests of hypothetical community.

(7) Frontier thinkers are those who have devoted a large part of their lives to the study of the science of education. These are the pioneers, the trailblazers, the theorists whose options are respected because of the nature of their work and experiences.

(8) *The "educational shortages" approach*. Sometimes surveys are made concerning the conditions in a community. The results of such surveys often reveal many deficiencies in the life of the community or in the social structure itself. These deficiencies or shortages are made as points or determinants in the selection of the curriculum content.

(9) *The "scissors-and-paste pot" approach*. This used to be the way courses of study were made during the early beginnings of public schools system. It consisted only of lifting bodily parts of courses of study in some schools in the United States and of putting them together almost without revision of alteration.

Current Trends in Curriculum Design and Organization

Before the curriculum could be used, the activities that go into it must be organized. The curriculum design and basis of organization however are selected in accordance with certain known principles.

Among the current trends in curriculum design and organization are the *following:*

(1) ***The Core Curriculum***. The core curriculum refers to one organized to provide a common core of learning, the core being a central idea around which is built experiences common to two or related subject fields. The core is a continuous sequence of a large, on-going experiences which contribute to better living in the home, school, and community. Accordingly, there are six types of core curriculum namely:

(a) ***Type one Core*** - is designed upon separate subjects, each taught independently. In this type an adopted set of textbooks is used for the basic materials of instruction and the so-called common needs are met largely by means of lessons from textbooks.

(b)   ***Type Two Core*** is a program design upon in formal correlations of subjects. The main characteristics of this type is its showing of the relationship between two subjects. Thus, when the history teacher is dealing with the Civil War, the English teacher might ask the pupils to read *"Uncle Tom's Cabin" or "Gone With The Wind."*

(c)   ***Type Three Core*** is a program design based upon systematic correlation. For example, the teachers of English, social studies, and science might agree that for a given period of time - say, six weeks - each would emphasize the same theme. Such a theme might be *"Living in the Home;"* the second six weeks of the semester might be given to *"Living in the Community."*

(d)   ***Type Four Core*** is correlated and fused program which offers enrichment of subject matter through its showing of the relationship to life of activities in the school, home, and community.

(e)   ***Type Five Core*** makes direct attack upon the needs of youth and the problems that beset them in present-day culture, through a program bridging the gap between education and life, between the curriculum and extra curriculum, and between general education and special education. In this type of core, Homeroom activities for the individual and the group become an integral part of the educative process as the teacher and pupils go about solving the problems.

(f) *Type Six Core* is a plan recognizing the dynamic characteristics of the learner and the learning process, providing for the optimum of teacher and student initiative, and for the use of the democratic process, guarding against *"freezing"* of programs in terms of problem areas or subjects to be mastered.

Definitions of the Core

(1) Core is defined as the organization within the experience curriculum of all those phases of experience which is felt should be common to all learners. It is also consist of those elements which make up good living in a democracy. The unit of work is a large on-going experience having a purpose which the pupils have accepted as their own.

(2) The Broad Fields Curriculum. Broad fields consist of a few areas each one cutting across lines traditionally dividing narrow subjects from one another.

Example of broad fields are:

a) Language Arts - Language, Reading, Spelling, Phonics, and Writing

b) Social Studies - History, Geography, Civics, Character Education, etc.

c) Home Economics - Foods, Nutrition, Clothing, Embroidery, *etc.*

d) English - Grammar, Poetry, Drama, Literature, Biography, Novel, *etc.*

e) Mathematics - Arithmetic, Algebra Geometry,

Physics, *etc.*

(3) The Separate Subjects or Correlated Subject Centered Curriculum. This is the traditional organization where subjects are taught separately. Correlation is done among subjects by bringing about a certain degree of unity among them in the recitation. The advantage of the separate-subject curriculum lies on the ease with which facts are systematized, organized, and evaluated. Its disadvantage lies in its compartmentalization which is psychologically unsound. Compartmentalization is not true to life. We do not ordinarily talk in terms of Language, Arithmetic, Reading, Science, and so on.

(4) Units of Work. The unit of work is the latest trend in curriculum organization. The principle behind this type of organization is wholeness, integration, and unity. The difference between a topic and a unit *(of work)* according to Monroe is that, a topic is in terms of subject matter. In contrast a unit *(of work)* is an organization of activities *(experience)* around a purpose *(problem)*.

THE UNIT

A unit is defined as an organized body of experience.

A unit is defined as *"an organized body of experience with a purpose meaningful to the child"* and accepted as his own which when carried out helps bring about a development of an integrated personality. There are three types of units, *namely:*

a) ***Subject - matter units.*** These include those ...

    (1)   organized around textbook chapters or topics.

    (2)   units organized around major generalizations, principles, or themes, and

    (3)   units organized around aspects of the environment such as air, water, sky, climate, *etc.*

b) ***Center - of - interest units*** - based on interests of pupils, on felt needs, on their dominant purposes, or on a combination of these.

c) ***Integrated experience units.*** These go further in seeking learning product which results in changed behavior and the adjustment of the individual.

A teaching unit is a plan that is developed by an individual teacher to be carried out in an individual classroom. Such unit may be of long or short duration depending on the subject or area which it deals at the age of the pupils, and other factors.

A resource unit is a collection of suggested teaching and learning activities organized around a given topic. Resource units are comprehensive in character so that they may be used on a selective basis. They are designed to provide materials which will be helpful to the teacher in developing teaching units.

The Activity Unit. According to Saucier, the activity unit is the only true experience unit. This is composed of a united series of activities about a central theme. The danger of activity unit lies in the tendency to over-emphasize the activity or movement at the sacrifice of the learning processes.

Characteristics of a Unit. The following are the lists of characteristics of a *unit:*

a)   The unit has a central theme around which the class work and activity revolve.

b)   The unit implies the use of more than one method of teaching. As the work activity changes so must the type of activity change.

c) The unit makes use of different kinds of learning activities of pupils.

d) The unit has common characteristics in its structure *namely:*

   1) A pre-test determines what the pupils already know about the unit.

   2) An overview which gives the learner the scope and purpose of the unit.

   3) A final test to find out how much a pupil has progressed as a result of it.

e) A unit requires a careful and advance preparation by the teacher.

The other characteristics of a unit are also listed as follows:

1) The unit should be based on purpose which is realistic for the children.

2) The unit should be one of a series which contributes to the total development of the learner.

3) A unit should deal with materials within the com-

prehension of the learner.

4) A unit should provide continuity in the development of the child.

5) A unit should deal with some phase or problem of living which is sufficiently significant as to merit careful study.

6) The unit should be one of a series which provides for a variety of activities or experiences for a class and a child as individual.

7) The unit should make provision that the data secured and the activities performed, including construction work should be as authentic as possible.

8) The unit should be cooperatively controlled by the group of learners and the teacher with the participation by the learners in all aspects.

Parts of a Learning Unit. There are three main parts of a learning unit, namely:

a) *Objectives.* These are the main goals of the learning activity.

b)　　*Activities*. A list of possible activities that children may do to realize the objectives. These actitivities may include research study from books and other written materials, illustration work including drawing, poster making, spattering, construction work, interviews of people, and the use of resource person and so on.

c)　　*Suggested outcomes*. These are the expected learning products. They may be in terms of knowledge, habits and skills, or attitudes and appreciations. In the development of units, the important thing to remember is not in the sequence of skills or activities, but in the sequence of experiences which promote the proper growth and the all-around development of the child.

Criteria in the Selection of Unit

a)　　It must be related to the concerns of the children.

b)　　It must be realistic. Experiences must be real and vital to the child.

c)　　It must have a wide range of activities.

d)　　It must contribute towards social understanding.

e)　　Unit experiences must be drawn from the basic

fields of human knowledge, such as the social studies, science, literature, and so forth.

f) It must lead to the growth of interests.

g) It must be provocative of the problem solving attitude.

h) It must be compatible with pupil's maturity.

i) It must be adopted to individual differences.

j) It must provide for continuity in learning experiences.

Means and devices for Selecting Materials for Instructional Purposes:

a) ***Survey***. Children make a list of the things that need improvement in the community. These are discussed in the class.

b) ***Field Trips***. These are guided observations outside the classroom.

c) ***Resource Persons***. Any person who specialized on a particular area or topic may be invited to tell the class about what he knows concerning that specialized area of topic.

d)   *Documentary Materials*. These refer to all written materials of special interest. It may include public records concerning an event of special significance, or to data gathered for statistical purposes, and the like.

e)   *Interview*. Pupils may interview people who can give them information about their work or about something they are working on.

f)   *Demonstration*. May be done by the teacher, by a resource person, or by a pupil who knows the method of doing something.

g)   *Work Experience*. This refers to a kind of employment pupils get out of the school during weekends, on vacations, or on off hours in factories, shops, or in the homes of people in the community. The nature of the job being an application of the theory or skill learned in school.

h)   *Questionnaires*. Children learn to make questions to be sent to people who are in a position to give the answer to certain things.

Tips on Obedience

"An alert child obeys quickly and accurately. Train yourself to listen carefully to your teacher's directions and to obey them to the letter. Inattention and stupi-dity are the reasons for most disobedience in class. If you cannot obey, your mind is too lazy to understand or too careless to wish to be polite. A slow muscle can be trained to act quickly."

"Soldiers are drilled to obey the least command without hesitation. Take pride in the discipline of your class, and obey like soldiers. Remember, that the less time there is wasted in collecting papers, opening and closing books, going to and from the board, the more time there is for study. And that is what you are sent to school for -- to study."

Areas of Community Living

There are eight areas into which learning is divided, namely:

a)   *Economic Security*. The average man needs freedom from want. To be free from hunger and want, the child who will some day be an adult should learn thrift or economy in the use of time, effort, and materials.

b)   *Peace and order*. The community group must learn to live together in peace. The child must learn to obey the laws of the school, the community, and the nation.

c)   *Hygiene and sanitation*. The community's health is the concern of everyone. The child should be taught good health habits.

d)   *Home beautification*. The beautifull home is a happy home. People must learn to improve their surroundings as well as the interior of their homes through knowledge of art.

e)   *Food production*. Every family and every home should be a store of plenty. Every child should an understanding or knowledge on how to produce food.

f)   *Recreation*. A man's life is not complete without any means means of relaxation. In school children should learn to play and participate in   games for purposes of enjoy-ment. Adults should learn to engage in hobbies or activities that may offer self-relaxation.

g)   *Civic life*. A good citizen should be concerned with the welfare of the group to where he belongs. He does nothing that will endanger or affect its welfare adversely.

h)   *Moral life*. We live in accordance to what we believe is right. Our customs, traditions, and culture determine what we ought to do and ought not to do.

The Philosophy of Integration

Integration is an abstract concept. It represents a process as broad as life itself. In education it means bringing about a state of unity through certain process that allows for the optimum development of the individual.

The concept of integration has been used to mean a variety of ways.

1) *Integration as a goal.* A state of perfect unity towards which effects ought to be directed.

2) *Physiological integration.* A process going on inside a living thing.

3) *Integration of behavior.* A process of adjustment to one's environment.

4) *Social integration.* A process by which a group of people and their culture becomes unified.

5) *Integrated courses.* Unification of subject matter from several related subjects.

6) *Integrated curriculum.* A curriculum pattern or way of organizing learning experiences to promote integration.

7) ***Integrated program.*** A completely unified activity program without subject matter division.

8) ***Integrated learning.*** Learning that enables the individual to act as an integrated whole.

9) ***Integrated experiences.*** The unified experiences of an individual.

10) ***Integrated teaching.*** An instructional process that seeks to bring about integrated learning experiences.

a) ***The Process of Integration.*** Integration is a harmonious interaction of the mental as well as the physical systems and processes. It also refers to harmonious interaction between the individual and his environment.

b) ***Two kinds of Integration***

1) *Personal Integration* - Perfect personal adjustment.

2) *Social Integration* - Perfect adjustment of the individual to his social goup. The ultimate aim of education is personal and social integration.

c) ***The Theory of integration in the Public Schools.*** Integration has often been wrongly used to mean a teaching process which follows a definite pattern, steps or procedures as practiced in some colleges. Integration, however, is not a method. It is a state of perfect unity or adjustment arising out of superior knowledge and control of diverging elements in a situation. Educator, no matter what the method is, aims at unity adjustment, hence, integration. But there are ways believed to be more effective in bringing about that unity and that is the so-called integrative process or integrative teaching technique. Integration is a philosophy based on the concept of freedom and respect of the individual personality. To the progressive, the child is the thing, the subject-matter is only important to the extent where it brings about the full development of the individual personality.

d) *Steps of the Integrative Method*

1) *Initiating the unit.* Pupils and teachers work together to begin a series of activities which are designed to accomplish a specific job. The teacher initiates the unit by creating a felt need, by an appeal to pupils' experiences, or by raising a series of problems bearing on a certain type of selected activity.

2) *Planning the Unit.* Under the leader-

ship of the teacher, pupils set down a plan of action to be followed by the class. The group is divided into smaller committees or groups for each certain aspect of the whole activity.

3) *Developing the Unit*. This is the actual work period. Pupils are assigned reference books or ask to consult reading materials for certain points, or problems studied or considered. Some may do construction work illustrative activities, or write reports, and so on, while others engaged themselves in other activities which have bearing on the total activity.

4) *Sharing Experiences*. Pupils share their experiences by means of reports, talks or other equally desirable means so that the rest will be acquainted regarding the group work.

5) *Culminating Activity*. Pupils culminate their work with something which is a natural result of the project such as a program, a demonstration, a party, etc.

Sources for the Selection
of Curriculum Materials

In addition to the approaches we mentioned there are other sources of materials from which we can build the curriculum, some of which may be mentioned in the *following:*

1)   ***Reports of national committees.***   National curriculum committees often report concerning certain changes in the curriculum. Such changes usually find their implementation in the field.

2)   ***Courses of study.*** The General Office issues from time to time courses of study in Language Arts, Arithmetic, Social Studies, etc. The courses of study are not issued to be followed lavishly, rather they are to be treated to serve as guides for teachers and school administrators.

3)   ***Textbooks.*** Textbooks like the course of study, are no longer the only source, but one of the many sources from which subject matter is to be taken.

4)   ***Trial and error.*** In the course of teaching, the teacher often resorts to trial-and-error. This is of course undesirable.

5)   *Teachers' opinions.* In the absence of an authority, the teacher's opinion often prevails after consideration has been made on children's needs and interests.

6)   *Opinions of selected groups.* Teachers often participate in workshop or work conferences and seminars. The opinions of the group often prevail.

7)   *Frequency of mention or space allotment.* Oftentimes, newspaper mention some particular needs, demands, or wishes. Such needs that were mentioned or the amount of space allotted to them in the press often indicate the necessity of including them in the curriculum.

8)   *Analysis of Social Activities.* Investigators analyzed human activities and grouped them into categories. These analysis are made as the basis of the curriculum.

9)   *Social processes.* Our relationships with one another in democracy are valuable sources of materials for the curriculum.

10)   *Natural Activities and references of children.* What children of certain groups and ages do or prefer to do indicate what should be taught to them.

11)   *Social, civic, and economic deficiencies.* Our

social defects or shortages, our civic duties that we often neglect, our economic faults - these could be analyzed and made use of in the curriculum.

12) *Generalizations*. What people generally believe to be good, pressing or right should find itself in the development of the curriculum.

13) *Current problems and issues*. Local or national problems concering politics, economics, and other burning issues of the day should be taken advantage of in the curriculum.

14) *Qualities of good citizens*. If we were to take not of the characteristics of a good citizen, we shall find out that we either have or do not have them. These qualities could be discussed and made use of in the classroom.

15) *Word list*. The Bureau of Public Schools has made a study of the most common words used by children by grades. The words indicate not only the frequency of use but also the level at which these words are used by children.

Resources of Learning

1) *Learning through community experiences.*

   a) Field trips.

   b) Interviews and visits of resource people.

   c) Service projects.

   d) School camping.

2) *Language through creative and socializing experiences.*

   a) Construction activities.

   b) Socialized experiences.

   c) Programs

   d) Clubs

3) *Learning through audio-visual experiences.*

   a) Objects, specimens, and models.

   b) Movies, theaters and the performing arts.

   c) Charts and graphs.

   d) Maps and globes.

   e) Copier and recorder.

   f) The radio and television.

4) *Learning through reading resources*.

    a) The text book, magazines and newspapers.

    b) Supplementary books.

    c) The elementary school library.

5) *Number of Experiences*.

    a) Development of number concepts.

    b) Development of quantative thinking.

    c) Use of actual number situations.

    d) Perception of sizes and comparison of objects.

    e) Perception of relationships of numbers, amounts and quantities.

    f) Development of insights.

6) *Scientific experiences*.

    a) Experiences about simple machines.

    b) Experiences about problems of nature.

    c) Experiences about changes in man's natural environment.

    d) Changes in man's social environment.

    e) Changes in man's intellectual life.

7) *Healthful experiences*.

    a) Maintaining one's health.

b) Development of health habits.

c) Health interests.

d) Personality development.

e) Safety problems or health hazards.

f) Common diseases.

g) Rest and sleep.

8) *Creative experiences.*

a) Drawing, poster making, illustrations, *etc.*

b) Construction work.

c) Entertainment and music.

d) Membership in a toy orchestra, *etc.*

Bibliography

Abitona A.B., Teaching Principles and Practices, Civil Service Reviewer, Compilation from Various Authors in Education

Avent J.E., The Excellent Teacher, Knoxville, Tennessee, 1931; pp. 183-193

Barr, A.S., *"Characteristic Differences in the Teaching Performance of Good and Poor Teachers of the Social Studies,"* Public School Publishing Company, Bloomington, Illinois.

Boardman, Charles, W., *"An Analysis of Pryil Ratings of High School Teachers,"* Educational Administration and Supervision, Vol. 15, pp. 148-354

Dewey, John, Experience and Education *(New York, The MacMillan Company, 1938),* Important Fields in Curriculum Making

Fraiser, George Willard, An Introduction to Education, Third Edition, Scott, Foresman and Company, Chicago, Atlanta, New York

Gate, A.I., Psychology for Students of Education, Revised Edition, Chapters I-V

Hyland Robert, E., S.J., The Catholic Philosophy of Education, *"Trends in Scholastic Teachings,"* Lecture Notes

Light, U.L., *"High School Pupils Rate Teachers,"* School Review, Vol. 38, pp.28-32

Lee, Murray, and Dorris May, The Child and His Curriculum, D. Appleton Century Company, Inc., pp. 3-3347

Klopp, W.J., *"Evaluation of Teacher Traits by Vacation School Pupils,"* School Review, Vol. 36, pp. 422-564

Knight F.B., *"Qualities Related to Success in Teaching, Contributions to Education,"* No. 120, Teachers College, Columbia University, New York City.

McMalion, James, J, S.J., *"Role of a Catholic Teacher,"* Lecture Notes

Peabody, Robert W., *"Pupil-Teacher Rating in Practice,"* School Executives Magazine, Vol. 50, pp. 191-192

Thorndike, E. L., Educational Psychology, Vol 1, Chapter 1; Principles of Teaching, Chapter 111; Instincts and Capacities; Elements of Psychology, Chapter XII

Woodworth, Robert S., Contemporary Schools of Psychology

ABOUT THE AUTHOR

The author is a self-made man. He is the youngest of ten well educated children who are in the field of engineering, medicine, dentistry, architecture, high ranking positions in the military, and in education. Both of his late parents were retired public school teachers and three of his elder siblings pursued the same profession in private schools and in professorial work.

Talented and persevering, he had the best that a student could reap from high school and college days. Won medals and citations for excellence in oratory, debate, and academic performances. His indomitable spirit has consistently sustained him even after college, in teaching life, when he etched his way towards a place under the sun.

From his stint as a U.S. Military in the law enforcement field, now a veteran, to the drug and alcohol counselor, research, training, and teaching assignments, it has always been a hard and painful way to the top. He has taught various subjects in the military including logistics issues, particularly about public safety. Being a mentor, however, hasn't killed the flair for writing which he has nurtured ever since his school days.

Unfazed by tight teaching schedules, he has written several articles, manuscripts, movie scripts, pamphlets and treatises especially on pedagogy and life. He has a degree in Public Administration, Criminology and Law, Masters (M.S. & M.A.) in Criminal Justice Administration and in Biblical Studies, and Doctorate (Ph.D.) in Administration of Justice and in Jurisprudence (J.D.) in late 70's to late 80's. A Cum Laude on his Bachelors, Magna and Summa Cum Laude on his Masterals. Formerly, a Director and Consultant in Research and Development for Education and Training Programs for La Salle Institute of Public Safety, Inc.

As a philantropist, the author intends to donate proceeds of this book to charities of worthy cause.

"No act of kindness, no matter how small, is ever wasted."

"Life is a race, a voyage, a growth, and a pilgrimage with a series of surprises ... it is a constant struggle, and without struggling, man cannot succeed."

Special Order Form
For Non-Credit Card Use

Send this order form with payment enclosed and payable to:

Edgar Cirilo Tandoc, LLC
Author • Publisher • Philantropist
Post Office Box 175 • Oroville, CA 95965 USA

Please send me the following books: *(All our books are in stock.)*

Qty. _____ **"Successful Teaching"**
ISBN 1451540795 @ **$15.95** each*

Qty. _____ **"America The Beautiful"**
ISBN 1451588143 @ **$19.95** each*

* Please add $5.43 for shipping and handling for each book.
Orders outside U.S. must be in U.S. funds.
Please print legibly.

Name: _____

Company (if applicable): _____

Address: _____

City: _____

State: _____ Zip: _____

Country (if outside U.S.) _____

Email: _____ Phone: _____

For orders outside the U.S., we will contact you for shipping cost adjustments if necessary. We encourage you to send a certified check or money order to avoid clearing time on personal checks. Books will be shipped via USPS with signature or delivery confirmation. *Need to order online?* Visit us at http://**www.EdgarCiriloTandoc.om**

Special Order Form

For Non-Credit Card Use

Send this order form with payment enclosed and payable to:

Edgar Cirilo Tandoc, LLC
Author • Publisher • Philantropist
Post Office Box 175 • Oroville, CA 95965 USA

Please send me the following books: *(All our books are in stock.)*

Qty. _____ **"Successful Teaching"**
ISBN 1451540795 @ **$15.95** each*

Qty. _____ **"America The Beautiful"**
ISBN 1451588143 @ **$19.95** each*

* Please add $5.43 for shipping and handling for each book.
Orders outside U.S. must be in U.S. funds.
Please print legibly.

Name: _____

Company (if applicable): _____

Address: _____

City: _____

State: _____ Zip: _____

Country (if outside U.S.) _____

Email: _____ Phone: _____

For orders outside the U.S., we will contact you for shipping cost adjustments if necessary. We encourage you to send a certified check or money order to avoid clearing time on personal checks. Books will be shipped via USPS with signature or delivery confirmation. *Need to order online?* Visit us at http://**www.EdgarCiriloTandoc.om**

You may photocopy the Special Order
Forms without tearing each page apart.

This book is available at special quantity discounts for bulk purchases for sales
promotions, premiums or fund raising. For details write to:

Edgar Cirilo Tandoc, LLC
Attn: Marketing Department
P.O. Box 175 • Oroville, CA 95965-0175

Email: info@edgarcirilotandoc.com

Or visit us online at http://**www.EdgarCiriloTandoc.com**

Thank You